THE HUMBLES

For other titles in the Target Series see end pages

THE HUMBLES

HILARY SETON

Target Editor: Mike Glover

Target Books is a division of Universal-Tandem Publishing Co., Ltd., 14 Gloucester Road, London SW7 4RD

First published in Great Britain under the title of 'Beyond the Blue Hills' by William Heinemann Ltd., 1973

First published in this edition by Universal-Tandem Publishing Co., Ltd., 1974

ISBN 0 426 10698 9

Printed in Great Britain by The Anchor Press Ltd., and bound by Wm. Brendon & Son Ltd., both of Tiptree, Essex

1

Grandfather Ganderglas not only repaired the greenhouses when the family moved into the Old House as caretakers; he added improvements which the family would not have dreamed of in years and years of dreaming.

'Look at these windows,' Grandfather Ganderglas commanded Aunt Tilly Humble, Coriander and Jan Humble, and their daughter, Araminta. 'When the greenhouses reach a certain temperature, these windows will fly open by themselves.'

'*Wonderful*, Grandfather,' breathed Araminta, longing to see the windows fly open by themselves.

'Very clever, father,' said Coriander, Araminta's mother, who much preferred windows to be opened and shut by people.

'Amazing,' said Jan Humble, Araminta's father, who was a poet and never properly appreciated Grandfather's inventions.

'Really practical,' said Aunt Tilly Humble, who knew what she was talking about. Tilly was a no-nonsense Humble.

'These windows aren't the end of the matter,' said Grandfather Ganderglas.

'Oh, dear,' murmured Coriander, 'inventors are very restless people to live with.'

Coriander didn't like change, even though she was Grandfather Ganderglas's daughter, and had been Coriander Ganderglas before she married Jan to become Coriander Humble.

'When these greenhouses reach a certain temperature,' Grandfather said again, 'the tomatoes will be automatically watered by sprinklers. The moment the right temperature is reached, the windows fly open and the sprinklers sprinkle.'

'Hear that?' demanded Aunt Tilly Humble of the others.

'Amazing,' said Jan for the second time, but he spoke so absently that Araminta knew a poem was being born. She watched her father's face anxiously. No one could ever be sure how the birth of a poem would take Jan Humble. Sometimes Jan's poems made him merry, sometimes they made him sad. Sometimes they went well, sometimes they didn't. Then Jan would sit hunched into himself, gloomy as O Misery Me, the Humbles' donkey.

'You'd better move your tomatoes into that greenhouse quickly, Grandfather Ganderglas,' said Aunt Tilly Humble, 'we're a good way into April already.'

'Aye,' said Grandfather, 'I'll move 'em this afternoon. Dinner first, though.'

'What are we having, Tilly?' asked Araminta.

'Pie, child.'

'What's in the pie, Tilly?'

'A plump wood pigeon stuffed with herbs for Grandfather Ganderglas and me; three eggs in young spinach for your father; bananas rolled in ham for you and your mother.'

Food was a subject on which the family never could agree. Jan ate only vegetables and eggs, nuts and fruit, cheese and honey. Birds and animals, he said, were his friends: he couldn't eat them.

Grandfather Ganderglas and Aunt Tilly Humble had no patience with him. A plump wood pigeon, a duckling stuffed with sage, a tasty morsel of chicken in rich gravy; there was always a succulence and richness and a savoury steam to the food that Grandfather and Tilly enjoyed.

Araminta and her mother, trying to keep the peace and be loyal to both sides, usually ended up with a bite of this and a bite of that.

'Come along, now,' said Aunt Tilly Humble, 'that pie will spoil.'

As they walked back to the house, Araminta whispered to her father: 'Is there a poem in your head?'

'Yes, Minty, yes, there is.'

A new poem. Minty loved a new poem.

'Tell me about your new poem, Father.'

'Later,' said Jan. He always said this.

'Just tell me what the poem's about,' pleaded Araminta.

'Caring,' said Jan.

'Caring?' repeated Araminta, astonished and disappointed. What sort of poem could that be? Jan usually wrote a poem you could get hold of. His best ones made you feel quite different from your ordinary self, setting your imagination on fire, showing you scenes and objects as you'd never seen them before: feelings, too. Jan was a great hand at poems about feelings. But caring!

'Not care*taking*, Minty,' Jan said, 'not what we're doing to this house, or only partly that. Caring comes into caretaking, but there's more to it.'

'We are not caretakers,' said Coriander, 'we are simply pausing here, and keeping an eye on the house while we do so.'

'We're being paid to see that the house is kept free of dust and burglars,' said Aunt Tilly, 'so we're caretakers. We answered an advertisement to be caretakers, so caretakers we are.' Aunt Tilly Humble did like to ram things home.

Araminta privately thought they were keeping the house company. Houses become lonely without people inside them. There's a sadness about a house where the windows are lighted from the outside by moonlight, instead of from the inside by lamps.

'We are not caretakers by trade or temperament,' insisted Coriander, 'Grandfather Ganderglas is an inventor, Jan's a poet, and I'm a herbalist.'

Araminta felt a little left out, and wondered whether Tilly did, too.

'Everyone has to be a bit of a caretaker in life,' said Grandfather Ganderglas.

'Exactly,' said Jan, 'that's what my poem is about. How everyone ought to care. Not just about houses. About everything.' Jan explained his thoughts better in poems than in conversation.

'I hope that pie won't have hardened,' said Aunt Tilly Humble.

'And since the only money we earn is by caretaking,' continued Grandfather, 'we're lucky to have a house worth taking care of.'

The family had fallen in love with the house even before they saw the wonder of its great curving staircase, or walked through the countless rooms and along the endless passages.

Coriander had only glimpsed the many ancient chimneys set on the old tiles of the roof when she had cried: '*There's* a house for you!' Coriander had very grand ideas.

'That house,' Jan had told Araminta, 'was built in the reign of Elizabeth the first.'

'If you ask me,' Tilly had remarked, 'we shall be dusting and polishing to the end of time before all the rooms in that house are as I'd like to see them.'

'There'll be some repairs to be done there all right,' said Grandfather, his eyes shining.

As for Minty, she had never seen such a house, with such a multitude of windows, all blinking gold in the evening sun.

'Now then,' said Tilly, 'don't start on about the house, or—'

'The pie will harden,' they all chanted.

Tilly pretended to be cross, and said if they weren't respectful, she would stop cooking for them.

How terrible that would be, thought Araminta, as they

crossed the terrace and edged into the hall round the great door, which had stuck, and would neither open properly nor shut.

'I'll have to see to that door,' said Grandfather Ganderglas.

How terrible, Araminta went on thinking, if Aunt Tilly Humble stopped cooking, and Grandfather stopped inventing, and father stopped writing poems, and mother stopped growing herbs, and she stopped, well, growing. And all at once she understood what her father was writing his poem about.

When the Humbles had gone into the house, the terrace looked lonely. The Humbles were like that. People might criticize them, call Jan feckless and Coriander proud, but any place was happier for their coming and poorer for their going.

The terrace looked neglected as well as lonely. Weeds were poking up between the stones, and a lot of the stones were cracked.

The balustrade, too, that separated the terrace from the lawns below, was broken in several places. Grandfather Ganderglas had put the terrace at the top of his list of Jobs that Needed Doing. There were a great many of these.

Inside the house, the Humbles were eating their pie in the great dining hall.

Aunt Tilly Humble had wanted the family to eat their meals in the kitchen, which was warm and cosy, but Coriander wouldn't agree.

'A dining room is to eat in,' said Coriander, 'however large.' Size was nothing to Coriander.

So they ate their pie sitting round the huge table. There were such big spaces between them that they had to raise their voices when they spoke. Not that anyone talked much.

Everyone was too busy eating pie; and thinking. The Humbles were great ones for thinking.

Grandfather Ganderglas was trying to make up his mind whether to move his tomatoes before or after seeing what was wrong with the door.

Aunt Tilly Humble, well pleased with her pie, was already wondering what to give the family for supper. Something light, she thought. A cherry flan, perhaps, using her last two jars of bottled cherries. Minty could fetch cream from the farm at the end of the lane.

'A jug of cream, child,' she said suddenly to Araminta, 'will you fetch a jug of cream from the farm this afternoon?'

Araminta said she would.

Jan Humble was thinking about his poem. Jan's poems started by twitching at the edges of his mind, and then moving in until he could think of nothing else. It wasn't fair of Aunt Tilly Humble to complain because he forgot about things like chopping wood or replacing a worn wick in a lamp or because he lost the shopping list when he went to the general store at Little Trumpington. No one could think of wood or wicks or shopping with a new poem taking up their every single thought.

Coriander said: 'Your best pie ever, Tilly.'

'*The* best pie ever,' agreed Jan, but he didn't speak with his heart. Minty knew his heart was with his poem. That was the worst of having a poet for a father. He was so often absent in spirit.

'You'd win a prize for pies any day, Tilly,' said Grandfather Ganderglas and his heart was in every word. Then he added: 'Takes a Humble to make a good pie.' The family laughed, but everyone knew Grandfather still hadn't quite succeeded. He had been trying for a long time now to make a joke about Humble and Pie but somehow the right wording always just eluded him.

Tilly was looking gratified and a little overcome. She never knew what to do with compliments and praise.

'Don't forget to feed O Misery Me, child,' she said to Araminta, by way of changing the subject.

'How is Misery?' enquired Jan. 'I haven't seen her today.'

'Gloomy,' said Minty. 'Gloomier than usual, even.'

'What Misery needs is a settled home,' said Grandfather.

This was what the family wanted, too. They needed to settle. They wanted a house of their own. Not just any house. Their caretaking activities had given them a taste for extravagant houses. They became cramped in body and mind when they couldn't walk about in a house without bumping into one another all the time.

Size wasn't all, however; the family needed more than just size.

There must be the right kind of room for Araminta: quite a small room, but up in the roof because Minty did like sleeping high, tucked into the eaves like a swallow.

Then there must be several big rooms for Grandfather Ganderglas, so that he could develop his inventions. Grandfather became crotchety and restless when he couldn't get on with his inventions. Just as Minty knew when there was a poem in Jan's head, so she knew when Grandfather Ganderglas was working up to another invention.

Then there must be a poetry-writing room for Jan, not too hot, not too cold, not too noisy, not too quiet. Jan said his thoughts clamoured too loudly in an absolutely quiet room.

Coriander must have a room, too, in which to make potions and ointments from her herbs.

Then there must be the right kind of kitchen for Aunt

Tilly Humble, who knew exactly what she wanted in the way of kitchens. She had a list of 'minimum requirements' as long as your arm.

There would have to be other rooms, of course, where the Humbles could be all together. Then they would also need a warm, sheltered garden where Coriander could grow herbs, and a field for O Misery Me, with a nice stout shed in one corner. O there was a lot to be considered. The Humbles were forever discussing the matter. Not just the kind of house and garden which they needed, but where to find the money to pay for them.

They began talking about this now.

'Perhaps you'll make a fortune with one of your inventions, Grandfather, and then you'll be able to buy a house,' said Araminta.

'Or Jan will become such a famous poet that the nation will give us a house in gratitude,' said Coriander.

'Meanwhile, we'd better make the best of being caretakers,' said Tilly, and that remark put a damper on their dreams all right. Sometimes, Tilly was too down to earth for comfort.

When the pie was finished, and the plates had been carried down the long passages to the kitchen, and washed up in the great stone sink, the Humbles went their different ways. 'See you at supper' they said to one another.

Minty had her afternoon all mapped out. Sometimes she liked to do this, and sometimes she liked to feel that a great, shining stretch of unused time lay in front of her. Anything could happen with unplanned time. She might see a bumblebee, or make a new friend. This afternoon, however, Minty knew exactly what would happen.

First, she would feed O Misery Me. She mixed Misery's dinner in a pail in the yard outside the kitchen.

The garden outside the kitchen was quite different from the garden by the terrace at the front of the house.

Outside the kitchen door, in the paved yard, there was a pump. The handle creaked, and the hinges were rusty, but the water that came wheezing out was bright and cold and sweet, quite, quite different from tap water.

The yard was enclosed by old stables. There hadn't been a horse in those stables for years and years. The family had cleaned one, and put fresh straw on the floor, so that Misery could spend the nights there. Behind the stables there was a walled-in kitchen garden, and behind the kitchen garden a little copse that led to Misery's meadow.

The kitchen garden was neglected like everything else, the blackcurrant bushes and redcurrant bushes and strawberries and gooseberries and rows and rows of vegetables all gone to seed. The greenhouses, which Grandfather Ganderglas had repaired and improved, were round this side of the house.

Araminta carried the pail past the stables, past the kitchen garden wall to the copse. Sometimes she walked through the middle of the wood, and sometimes she walked along the edge. Today, she walked through the middle, counting toadstools as she went. She counted thirty-two before she noticed the first primroses she had seen that year, and forgot about toadstools.

Soon there would be bluebells. Araminta wondered whether there might be cowslips. Cowslips were her favourite flower. There was nothing, nothing, nothing in the world, thought Minty dreamily, as she walked along, like the smell of a bunch of cowslips.

The wood was small, but the trees grew close together so that the sun stayed outside. There was a warm, dark smell. Minty could never decide whether she liked the inside of the wood or not. She liked the primroses, she liked the toadstools, and the pine needles to walk on, and the strong, heady, resinous smell of pine, but she wished a little more sun could push through the trees. The wood was really very dark. And except for the occasional rustling of invisible animals, very silent. Minty understood what her father meant by too much silence; very silent places suddenly showed you all your thoughts at once.

She saw little spears of sunshine lying on the ground in front of her, and knew she was coming to the end of the wood. She walked more quickly. In a moment or two she would see Misery's field and Misery standing in the corner, where she always stood, hunched against an oak tree.

The Humbles had bought O Misery Me from some gypsies because she looked so sad. She wrung the heart of everyone who looked at her. To start with, she stood with such a dismal droop, one little back leg bent and her head hanging right down. And when she did raise it she looked at you with beautiful, gentle eyes absolutely brimming with sorrow. When she had looked at the Humbles like this they had been convinced that the gypsies treated her badly. No donkey could be well treated and look so sad, they thought. The gypsies had been very angry when they learned what the Humbles suspected. They treated that donkey very well, they said, they were exceptionally kind to her. She simply had a melancholy disposition and that was that.

The Humbles felt sure they could cheer her up, but so far they hadn't managed to. Being sad didn't make Misery less beautiful. She was the colour of a dark conker, except for her face, which was lighter, and the faint tracing of a cross on her back, which was darker. The only part of Misery that wasn't beautiful was her tail. She had a thin,

limp, draggly tail and it hung like a broken bell rope.

'I've a lovely dinner for you, Misery,' said Minty in a coaxing voice.

The Humbles all seemed to think that because Misery had a melancholy disposition she must be delicate. In fact, she was rather strong.

Misery sniffed her dinner and ate a mouthful. She didn't always eat much at a time, and usually Araminta left the pail with her; but today she sat down beside her and told her the family news while she ate. Then, when at last Misery had finished, she patted her strong, soft neck and carried the empty pail back to the house. Misery looked after her in a melancholy kind of way.

Araminta carried the empty pail back to the yard, and scrubbed it clean with water from the pump. The door to the kitchen was open, and Minty could see Aunt Tilly Humble making the pastry for her cherry flan. Minty knew that when she saw her, Tilly would call: 'Don't forget to fetch the cream from Mrs Figge at the farm, child.'

As Minty gave Misery's pail a final swill with pump water, Tilly called: 'Don't forget the cream, child.'

'I'll go when I've looked at Mother's herb garden,' Araminta called back.

'So long as you don't forget.' Tilly was always on the alert lest Minty should grow into a dreamy, poetic Humble instead of a practical, no-nonsense Humble.

Araminta put Misery's pail beside the pump, washed her hands and set off to find Coriander.

The herb garden was beyond the lawns at the front of the house. Coriander had been very pleased to find one already laid out. She kept telling Araminta how it had been there for nearly four hundred years, though no one seemed to have bothered with it for at least a hundred, judging by the weeds and the height of the box hedges round the beds. Coriander had spent days preparing the soil and chopping the hedges to the proper height. Coriander said she had never seen a herb garden so neglected.

As Minty crossed the terrace, she saw Grandfather Ganderglas trying to discover what was wrong with the front door. He looked totally engrossed so Minty didn't disturb him. She walked on down the flight of crumbling steps to the grass below.

The herb garden was behind a high hedge. At first sight, the hedge looked solid, but there was a small gate, very low down, right in the middle. When Minty reached the gate, she could see her mother, kneeling by one of the beds.

Coriander was planting. All the Ganderglas family were herbalists, except Grandfather, who had confused everyone by turning into an inventor. One Ganderglas had been a doctor, a real doctor, with a waiting room and bottles of pink medicine.

Coriander hadn't really liked having to be Coriander Humble instead of Coriander Ganderglas, although she wouldn't have said so to Jan. She loved Jan more than she minded his name, but being called Humble didn't suit Coriander at all. 'That's what love does for you,' she would sigh to Araminta, 'gives you a name like Humble.'

Araminta did rather hope that when love came to her it might carry a rich-sounding name, though she, too, was careful never to say this aloud for fear of hurting Jan's feelings.

'Hullo,' called Araminta to her mother, 'what have you planted?'

'I've planted thyme and lemon thyme,' Coriander told her, 'mint and parsley; fennel and tarragon, coriander and—'

'Coriander!' cried Minty. 'That's your name. I didn't know you were a herb, Mother.'

'Every Ganderglas is named after a herb,' said Coriander.

'Why didn't you call me after one?' asked Araminta. 'I'm partly Ganderglas.'

'Because Jan was so set on calling you Araminta.'

'Well, Minty is a little bit herby, isn't it? What else are you planting?'

'Wood betony, saffron, southernwood, hyssop, lovage. . .'

'What are they all used for?' asked Araminta.

'Mint for earache, parsley for coughs, fennel for hiccups,' chanted Coriander, 'wood betony for rheumatism and indigestion; saffron for gout; southernwood draws out splinters, hyssop for dropsy and lovage for pleurisy.'

'Have you a favourite herb, mother?'

'I'm very fond of balm,' Coriander said. 'The great Culpeper, who knows all there is to know about herbs, says that balm should be kept in every house to relieve the weak stomachs and sick bodies of poor and sickly neighbours.'

'Our only neighbours are the Figges, and they're not poor or sickly, are they?' observed Minty.

Coriander looked dark at mention of the Figges. Coriander had offended Mrs Figge almost as soon as she had met her by offering her an ointment made from wild thyme to cure her warts. Mrs Figge wouldn't dream of admitting she had any.

'Are there witches in the Ganderglas family, mother?' asked Minty.

'Certainly not,' said Coriander, 'only herbalists and healers. Not that I've anything against white witches, but there are only herbalists in the Ganderglas family.'

Araminta loved herbs. She loved their names, and the way they smelled, and the long history of their use in medicine and cooking; she loved helping Coriander to stuff little muslin bags with lavender and thyme to put among their clothes.

'Can I help you?' she asked.

'Not at the moment, thank you Minty.' Coriander always said this. She never wanted help with her herbs.

Araminta visited her father next. When the days were warm, Jan wrote his poems beside the lily pond, and today was warm. Araminta walked across the lawns. Jan looked just as absorbed as Grandfather Ganderglas had done, and Araminta didn't know whether to disturb him or not. So she stopped a short distance away and watched him.

'Aren't you coming any nearer?' called Jan presently.

Araminta walked up to him. 'I thought you were too busy with the poem to talk,' she said.

'Daughters are more important than poems,' replied Jan. 'I'd stop whatever I was doing for you, Minty.'

'Would you?' said Araminta, quite surprised and very pleased. Being told that she was more important than a poem gave her a new idea of herself. She never quite knew where she stood in life. If she was more important than a poem to Jan, did this mean she was more important than a herb to Coriander, or an invention to Grandfather Ganderglas, or a pie to Aunt Tilly Humble?

'Have you finished your poem?' asked Araminta.

'Oh no, not nearly.'

'Will you sell it, when you have?'

'If I can.'

Araminta could never understand why people wouldn't buy poems. Father wrote lovely poems but papers and magazines only occasionally bought them. Sometimes he wrote them out in his best writing, and sold them for two pence a sheet. Mostly, he gave them away. Poets have everything to recommend them except being absent in spirit and not making money.

Grandfather Ganderglas became very exasperated when Jan gave away his poems. He wouldn't dream of giving anyone an invention. Coriander wasn't much better, said Grandfather; she was forever giving people potions made from her herbs to help them slim, or sleep, or grow more hair, or improve their nerves. 'Sell them, my girl, sell them,' he would say, and Aunt Tilly Humble quite agreed with him.

Araminta couldn't become used to hearing her mother called a girl. Coriander was very beautiful, but she had stopped being a girl when she had found true love—and changed her name from Ganderglas to Humble.

'Will you read me your poem?' asked Araminta.

'Not yet.'

Father always said this. He never would read out his poems.

'I'll go and see Grandfather now,' said Araminta, feeling shy suddenly. She was still overcome at learning that she was more important to her father than a new poem. She felt as Tilly had done when the family praised her pie, and so pleased that she ran very fast across the grass to Grandfather Ganderglas, who was still busy with the door.

'Have you found out what's wrong?' asked Araminta.

'Aye,' said Grandfather Ganderglas, 'just watch how this door opens and shuts now.'

Araminta watched as Grandfather swung the great door to and fro.

'Marvellous, Grandfather.'

'I'll move my tomatoes now,' said Grandfather.

'Would you like any help?'

'No, thank you, Minty, the boxes are too heavy for you.'

No one needed her help, Minty thought, except Tilly, who wanted her to fetch the cream. She walked with Grandfather round to the potting shed, where Grandfather had put his tomatoes while he mended the greenhouse.

'Grandfather, who does this house belong to?'

'A fine gentleman called Richard Arthur Edmund Cressington.'

'Richard Arthur Edmund Cressington,' repeated Araminta in wonderment. There was a name for you. Four names. What could anyone want with four names? Still, she wished now she had an extra one or two herself.

'Why doesn't Mr Cressington live here?'

'We were told he travels too much to live anywhere for long.'

'Who told you?'

'The solicitor who gave us the caretaking job. He looks after Mr Cressington's business.'

'What's a solicitor?' and then Araminta held her breath because Grandfather didn't like too many questions.

Grandfather ruminated. Then he said: 'I suppose you might say a solicitor makes life official.'

'Might you?' said Araminta, who had no idea what he meant.

'A solicitor,' said Grandfather, 'turns life into a blob of sealing wax. A solicitor won't let folk be born or live or die without drawing up a lot of conditions, and making arrangements, and dropping on sealing wax, and charging money.'

Araminta could see that Grandfather didn't care for solicitors.

They had reached the greenhouse now, and Grandfather went inside, so there was no more to be learned from him about Richard Arthur Edmund Cressington.

Araminta walked on. She walked down the drive and out of the gates, and into a long, narrow, curving lane shaded by elm trees.

There were rooks' nests at the top of the trees. In the evening the sky grew dark with rooks coming home. And the noise! Such a chattering and cawing. Minty preferred swallows. She was waiting very anxiously for May to follow April so that she could find out whether swallows would come to the Old House. Swallows or swifts or martins, Minty didn't mind; she loved them all. She loved the speed with which they screeched and swooped and raced about the sky. Lovely happy swallows. They brought the summer and, when they left, they seemed to take it away again.

The Figges lived at the end of the lane. They were renowned for being hard workers. Mr Figge was hardly ever to be seen, he worked so hard, and Mrs Figge was endlessly on the bustle. They made Minty feel a little dizzy. Even Aunt Tilly, who was reckoned to be the hardest worker in the living memory of the Humbles, stopped sometimes to rock in her chair by the window, or knit, or read Araminta a story, or even to have a game of Hunt the Silver Thimble. Mrs Figge would have scorned to stop for five minutes.

When Araminta reached the farm, she saw only Wag, a black and white collie. Minty liked Wag best of the Figge family. He was never too busy for a game, or a walk on the downs. Mr Figge said Wag was a lazy, no-good dog, and not a patch on his two brothers, who were the best dogs with sheep Mr Figge had ever known.

Araminta had a short chasing game with Wag, then went

to the dairy. Mrs Figge, busy making her special cheese, saw her coming.

'Hullo, Araminta,' she said, 'you'll be wanting cream, I daresay?'

'Yes, please,' said Minty, 'Aunt Tilly Humble is making a cherry flan.'

'Your Aunt Tilly Humble is as skilful a cook as I've met,' said Mrs Figge, and she wasn't one to give praise lightly. 'Have you brought a jug with you?'

'Sorry,' said Araminta, 'I forgot.'

'Forgot!' scolded Mrs Figge. 'A little girl like you with nothing to remember. Shame on you, Araminta Humble. Don't forget to bring this back now'—and she took a big, brown, earthenware jug from the shelf above her head. She had strong, sunburned arms.

'No, I won't forget,' Araminta promised. 'I'll bring it back tomorrow.'

'My regards to your Grandfather and your Aunt Tilly Humble.' After a pause she added: 'And your mother and father.' Mrs Figge had more to say to Grandfather and Aunt Tilly on account of their being the practical ones of the family. Apart from having felt annoyed with Coriander for drawing attention to warts she knew she didn't possess, Mrs Figge thought Coriander proud, and impractical over what mattered in life. Mrs Figge didn't think herbs mattered.

'Goodbye, Mrs Figge,' said Araminta.

'Be careful not to spill that cream now, and remember to bring back the jug.'

Minty walked back along the lane. Wag came part of the way with her. He barked when they passed the half hidden chalk track that led up to the downs, but Minty explained she couldn't walk on the downs just now. Wag returned to the farm, looking disappointed.

Tilly was still in the kitchen. She was setting the iron kettle to boil on the hob. The family drank a lot of tea; in addition to ordinary tea, they often had Coriander's herb tea.

'That's a lovely looking cherry flan,' Minty said. 'Here's the cream, and Mrs Figge sent you her regards.'

'And be good enough to take mine to her when you return that jug. Why didn't you take one of ours?'

'I forgot,' said Araminta, and was scolded all over again.

When Tilly heard the lowing of the cattle as Mr Figge drove them down the lane, she knew the time must be six o'clock: so she sent Minty to remind the family about the cherry flan. Much though the Humbles enjoyed their food, they always had to be reminded about meals.

Later, when the April evening was beginning to grow dark and the lamp on the supper table was glowing the brighter because of this, Grandfather Ganderglas lighted Minty's own little lamp and she kissed each of the family goodnight.

To reach her bedroom, Minty climbed stairs and turned corners, walked along passages and climbed more stairs. Minty's room was so high and small and remote that she felt like a princess in a tower. When she reached it, she set down her lamp on her table and looked from her window over the darkening land and up to the tiny stars that had begun peppering the sky. And that was the end of a usual sort of day for Minty: until she met the Minders, that is. She met the first of them the very next day.

2

The day started with one of Aunt Tilly Humble's efficient moods, one of her 'let's have a good scrub and dust' moods. Whenever this happened, the rest of the family at once remembered urgent jobs of their own. Tilly was apt to say 'There's work here for everyone', and no one wanted that kind of work.

Coriander murmured something about her herbs as she hurried out, and Jan slipped after her without any excuse at all. Grandfather Ganderglas said he wanted to borrow some seed boxes from Mr Figge the farmer; so Tilly told him to take the jug back.

Minty crept out of the back door very quietly. She thought she might have a quick look at the greenhouse while Grandfather was calling on Mr Figge, and then take Misery up to the downs. Perhaps she would call for Wag on the way.

The greenhouse looked quite different now that Grandfather had filled it with growing plants. Minty was amazed at the vigour of Grandfather's plants, so early in the year. They were climbing up strings to the roof. She opened the greenhouse door and closed it behind her. There was a warm, moist smell and a faintly green tinge to the air.

Araminta liked being in the greenhouse. The day was cold, even though they were nearly in May. She sat down on Grandfather's chair, and then jumped up again. Someone had spoken to her. Spoken quite sharply. And there was no one in the greenhouse except herself.

'Excuse me,' the voice had said, 'but you're sitting on my hat.'

Araminta stared all round: she saw only tomatoes. So she decided that somehow she must have imagined the voice and sat down once more on Grandfather's chair.

'You're sitting on my hat *again*,' cried the voice, sounding absolutely amazed at such behaviour. 'My *new* hat.'

'I *am* sorry,' said Araminta, leaping off the chair. When she looked down she saw she had been sitting on a hat, a small purple trilby which she had squashed completely flat. She began pushing it back into shape and hoped the owner couldn't see the damage she had done.

'I *think* your hat will be all right,' she said, wishing she knew who she was talking to.

'I certainly hope so. I've only had it a fortnight.'

'I'm afraid I can't see you,' said Araminta.

'Perhaps you need spectacles.'

'Where should I look?' asked Minty, ignoring the remark about spectacles. She thought that finding the owner of the voice was harder even than playing Hunt the Silver Thimble.

'There's no point in gazing at the roof,' said the voice. 'You usually find people on the ground, don't you?'

Araminta looked down and saw, half hidden behind Grandfather's largest plant, a small, fat man sitting on a camp stool. He had red shiny cheeks, exactly like two ripe tomatoes, and wore a crumpled green suit.

'Good morning,' he said, 'I'm Horace Tompkins and I'm a bachelor.'

'Good morning,' said Minty, 'I'm Araminta Humble, and I'm sorry I sat on your hat.'

'We all make mistakes,' said Horace Tompkins.

There was an awkward pause.

'Excuse me asking,' said Araminta finally, 'but what are you doing in Grandfather's greenhouse, sitting by his tomatoes?'

'The tomatoes may belong to your grandfather; my information is that the greenhouse doesn't. I'm told that your family are the caretakers here.'

'Yes, that's right, but Grandfather mended these greenhouses,' Minty told Horace Tompkins. 'When a certain temperature is reached the windows fly open and the sprinklers sprinkle.'

'I shall soon put a stop to that,' declared Horace, 'I don't intend to get soaked every five minutes.'

'Do you mean to stay then?'

'For a while. You'll always find a Tompkins where there are tomatoes just as you'll always find a Larchington where there's timber. I shall stay for a while though, mark you, if I'd known how your Grandfather's tomatoes were flourishing I should never have come.'

'Why not?' asked Minty.

'The Minders only move in where there's neglect and there's none here. I was told the old greenhouses were falling to pieces, and what do I find but the most flourishing plants I've ever seen? Still, I shall stay awhile—when the Minders move in, they move in.'

'Who are the Minders?' asked Araminta.

'The Minders,' said Horace Tompkins, 'are people who mind, who look after things, sometimes in a practical way, sometimes in a caring way.'

'I think Father's written a poem about you then.'

'Most obliged I'm sure,' said Horace Tompkins.

'Are there many Minders?' asked Minty.

'We're dwindling, I'm afraid, compared with what we once were. Once there were Minders all over the land. When the Minders' Reunion was held, you would think a dozen armies had gathered together. There were families and families, all large. There are still a good few of us, but nothing compared with the old days. And not enough for all the work there is to do. People seem to care less and less as the Minders become fewer and fewer.'

'Is Mr Larchington anywhere near here?'

'Yes, he is as it happens. He's in Farmer Figge's forest. You may have seen him with his saw. Not that Jim would ever use his saw on living wood, mark you; he's more interested in growing trees than in cutting them down, but he feels very strongly about people leaving dead wood lying about to rot. That's pure waste, Jim says, and I agree with him.'

'I haven't seen him,' said Minty, 'but I haven't been to Mr Figge's forest yet.' She sat down again, but was careful to put Horace's hat on a shelf.

'Where do you live, Mr Tompkins?'

'On the job mostly. Of course, with some of us, myself for instance, the job's seasonal, but forests and plantations keep Jim busy all the year. Some jobs do, some don't. Take Fred Steeple. The Steeples keep an eye on churches, and there's always something to mind in a church, whatever the season.'

'But where do you live when you are not on the job?' persisted Araminta.

'In the Village.'

'What village?'

'The Village.'

Araminta thought this a very strange answer. She knew there were hundreds of villages.

'What's the name of this village?'

'It's too famous to need a name,' said Horace Tompkins. 'Everyone knows about the Minders' Village.'

'Are the Minders famous?'

'Some are. Nathaniel the Clockmaker, for instance.'

'Why is he famous?'

'I've had enough questions for the moment,' said Horace.

Araminta was disappointed. She would have liked to learn more about Nathaniel and the Minders' Village.

'Would you like to be introduced to my mother and father and Grandfather Ganderglas and Aunt Tilly Humble?'

'All in good time,' said Horace.

'Can I meet Mr Larchington and Mr Steeple?'

'All in good time,' said Horace.

Minty wondered what time meant to Horace Tompkins. To some people a phrase like 'all in good time' meant this year, next year, sometime, never.

'Will you tell me about the Village and the Minders if I come back again?'

'I might,' said Horace.

When Araminta reached the house she saw Grandfather coming towards her and wondered whether he would notice Horace Tompkins when he went into the greenhouse: or whether Horace would speak to him.

'Hullo, Araminta,' called Grandfather, 'all well in the greenhouse?'

'I think so.'

'Only think?' said Grandfather. 'Aren't you sure?'

'The tomatoes are growing,' said Minty and skipped away, across the yard to the open kitchen door. She looked cautiously through the doorway. She didn't want to find herself taking part in Tilly's clean-up.

Tilly was talking to Jan in the kitchen and Araminta wondered whether she was trying to persuade him to do a spot of dusting.

'Can I take Misery for a walk?' she called.

'That child,' said Aunt Tilly Humble, 'ought to be at school.'

'You know the arrangement was that I should teach Minty myself,' Jan said. 'I have official permission to do so.'

'But you never do teach her,' said Tilly, 'she spends all day doing nothing; and you're not much better. The sooner you realize that poetry isn't a way of life, Jan Humble, the better for all of us.'

'Well, I'll teach her now. Come along Minty, we'll have a lesson.'

'What kind of lesson, Father?'

'I haven't thought yet.'

'You see how unorganized you are,' said Tilly. 'You never do give the matter a thought, that's the trouble. That child needs regular lessons. I shall draw up a timetable. That was the arrangement we made when the man came.'

The man had come a long way to see the Humbles. He said he had been looking for them for months. He was softly spoken, that man, and carried a case full of official papers. He had come to say that Minty ought to go to school. The Humbles had disliked him on the spot. They replied that they could teach Minty themselves, and the argument had gone on all the evening. Finally, the man had agreed to let the family teach Araminta on condition she had regular lessons.

Tilly reminded Jan of this. 'Regular lessons, the man said, Jan. We must remember that. I shall teach her to cook and to clean; Grandfather Ganderglas can teach her sums; you can teach her to read and to write and Coriander can teach her about herbs.'

'I know some of the herbs,' said Minty, 'I know that devil's-bit scabious has purply flowers near the end of summer and cures coughs and fevers and scurf-itch, pimples and freckles. Wild angelica for colic; adderstongue for wounds, squirting cucumber for—' She stopped. What could squirting cucumber be used for?

'There, Tilly,' said Jan, 'what other child of Minty's age knows all that?'

'There's more to life than herbs, Jan Humble, just as there's more to life than poetry, and that child needs regular lessons.'

'Well, come along, Minty, come and have a regular lesson,' said Jan, laughing.

Minty knew that while Coriander wanted her to be a herbalist and Tilly wanted her to be a cook and needlewoman and Grandfather Ganderglas wanted her to be handy with tools, Jan only wanted her to be herself. She loved Jan for this.

'Father,' she said, as they walked away, 'have you heard of people called Minders?'

'Yes, yes, I have Minty, they're a greatly respected people. They move in when there's been neglect. At one time every town and village and hamlet, even, in the land had a Minder who visited regularly, but there are not enough of them now.'

'And have you heard of their Village?'

Jan nodded. 'The Village is within a couple of days walking from here. But no one ever reaches it unless they are shown the way by a Minder.'

'Why not?'

'The path twists and turns among and between and over and around the Blue Hills and often it disappears altogether.'

'Where are the Blue Hills?'

'At the edge of the Empty Plain.'

'Where's the Empty Plain?'

'You have to follow the chalk path up to the downs until you reach the great ox drove, and you follow that for miles and miles until you arrive at the Hilltop Town; from the Hilltop Town you look down on the Empty Plain and at the far side of the plain, where it begins to rise into the Blue Hills there's a signpost pointing over the Winding Way to the Minders' Village.'

'Have you tried to find the way, Father?'

'No, Minty.'

'Your new poem, the one about caring; that's what the Minders do, isn't it?'

'How did you learn about the Minders, Minty?'

Araminta's cheeks grew pink. She had never had a secret from Jan, and she had never told him anything that wasn't true; but, for the moment, she wanted to keep Horace Tompkins secret.

'Do you mind,' she asked, 'if I tell you later on?'

'Whenever you like,' said Jan, but he sounded a little sad.

The family never had much of a midday meal when Tilly had one of her efficient moods on. Today she gave them cheese and salad, which suited Jan all right, but Grandfather Ganderglas muttered that he wasn't a mouse, or a rabbit, either. Then he forgot all about what he was eating and said would they believe it, when he had gone into the greenhouse, he had found the sprinklers turned off. He asked Minty whether she had been playing with them.

'No, I didn't touch the sprinklers,' said Minty, and changed the subject. 'May I take Misery to Mr Figge's forest this afternoon?'

Grandfather said that he and Farmer Figge were going there themselves because Figge wanted to look at some of his young trees; so they could all go together.

Araminta felt disappointed. She didn't think she had much chance of finding Jim Larchington if she was with Grandfather Ganderglas and Mr Figge. Then Coriander asked her to look for any sweet woodruff that might be flowering early; Coriander said she just fancied a cup of woodruff tea.

'What does woodruff look like?' asked Minty and Coriander told her to look for a plant about a foot high with white, bell-like flowers and a sweet smell. 'Good for the stomach and liver,' added Coriander from force of habit, 'and for encouraging appetite.'

'No need for that in this family,' said Grandfather Ganderglas, 'when Aunt Tilly Humble does the cooking.'

When Minty fetched O Misery Me from her field, she whispered into one of her long ears: 'Do have a good look round for Jim Larchington when we reach the forest, Misery.' Misery blew down her nostrils and rubbed her nose against Araminta's hand.

The Humbles did have an old saddle and bridle for Misery, but they were never used. Araminta just climbed on her back and told her which way to go. If she went in a hopelessly wrong direction, Araminta would slide off and set her right and then climb back. Today, Grandfather would be there to guide her.

First they went along the lane to the farm to meet Mr Figge. Misery walked slowly. She had delicate legs and the dearest little hooves.

Wag was looking out for them. When he saw them, he barked a loud welcome and waved his feathery tail.

Mr Figge came stumping out of the yard into the lane. He was a stumping kind of man. He wore gaiters on his stout legs and generally had a leather jerkin hanging open over his shirt. 'Afternoon, Ganderglas,' he called to Grandfather, then nodded to Minty and smote Misery on her flank. Misery looked the other way.

They walked back along the lane until they reached the chalk path that led up to the downs. Then Grandfather guided Misery up the path, Mr Figge walked behind and Wag raced up and down, keeping everyone together. The only time he ever did any rounding up was when he had people to look after.

The chalk path climbed higher and higher until it reached

the great ox drove, a track that stretched along the ridge for countless miles in either direction; but their way lay over, not along, the ridge, down to the forest. First, they looked down on to the trees and then they were among them—beech and pine, spruce and fir, with here and there the silver-grey shiver of a whitebeam.

'Just listen to those birds,' said Grandfather, and Minty, when she listened, heard the cooing of wood pigeons, and the harsh cry of a jay and the haunting, plaintive call of the peewit.

At the foot of the downs, between Mr Figge's trees, there was a valley path known as Washers Pit, which led to the village of Little Trumpington. When they reached this path, Araminta slid off Misery's back and let her wander off. Misery did love to browse among bushes and grasses, trying a mouthful of this and a mouthful of that.

'Keep that donkey off my young trees,' called Mr Figge, but he spoke absently. He and Grandfather were already absorbed in looking at the trees and talking about them.

Mr Figge sold Christmas trees at Christmas time, logs for fires in winter, pea sticks in spring and wood all the year round for building and general purposes.

Minty looked to see if any sweet woodruff might be growing anywhere near, but she only saw primroses and a general spring bursting.

Some of the trees weren't out properly. Their leaves were still sepia-coloured and tightly curled. Other trees were already green, a brilliant spring green which looked all the brighter because of the dark pines.

Mr Figge was telling Grandfather what a good investment the trees were, and Minty thought that if the trees were hers she wouldn't sell any; perhaps she would give away a few Christmas trees, but the others would just stay and grow and she would watch their spring leaves unfurl into a summer fullness, and then watch autumn change their colour and then see winter sweep them bare.

Minty liked winter trees. As Grandfather said, you could really see the shape of a tree in winter. She had never heard Mr Figge talk about the shape of a tree; only about the value.

Minty had heard Coriander say that Mr Figge would never give away so much as a fir cone; so when they all heard a cry of 'Timber', and saw pine logs rolling down between the trees following and bumping one another right down to the path, Mr Figge couldn't believe his eyes.

'Hey,' shouted Mr Figge, but that didn't stop another cry of 'Timber', and another dozen logs rolling down almost to their feet.

'Come on, Ganderglas,' cried Mr Figge, 'I'm not having this,' and he raced up into his trees, followed more slowly by Grandfather.

Araminta followed Grandfather.

When they reached Mr Figge, he was shouting at a man as straight as a pine, though nothing like so tall; he was small and slight.

'Who d'you think you are?' shouted Mr Figge for the tenth time, 'and what d'you think you're doing? And why are you carrying a saw?'

'My name is Jim Larchington, and generally speaking I keep an eye on your trees; at this particular moment I'm rolling pine logs.'

'What d'you mean, "keep an eye on my trees"? I look after my trees.'

'Oh, I don't think so,' said Jim Larchington politely, 'you're hardly ever here, are you? You only come when there's a sale to be made, or a tree to be felled or one to be planted. On and off, I'm here most of the time, seeing they're not diseased or overcrowded and all the rest of it.'

'Then you're trespassing,' roared Mr Figge, 'and I shall have you arrested.'

Jim Larchington just smiled. His jacket was the colour of a tree's bark and his boots the colour of moss: he was dressed in neither green nor brown, but a woody mixture of the two.

'Washers Pit is a right of way,' Grandfather reminded Mr Figge, 'it leads to Little Trumpington. He's not trespassing on a right of way.'

'He's off the right of way, he's among the trees, *my* trees, he's holding a saw in his hand, he's been rolling pine logs. *My* logs. Here they are in evidence.'

Minty thought things weren't going too well for Jim

Larchington, so she said: 'Mr Larchington is a Minder. I met his friend, Mr Tompkins, in your greenhouse, Grandfather, and he's one, too. He told me I might find Mr Larchington here.'

'We shall have to take action, Ganderglas,' said Mr Figge, speaking grimly, 'it's quite clear to me these fellows are worse even than trespassers. They're squatters.'

'Mr Tompkins did say that when the Minders move in they move in,' agreed Minty.

'I've heard of the Minders,' said Grandfather, 'but I didn't know there was one in my greenhouse. Why didn't you tell me, Minty?'

'I asked Mr Tompkins if he would like to be introduced to you, Grandfather, and he said "all in good time".'

'And did Mr Tompkins turn off my sprinklers?' demanded Grandfather.

'I expect so. He told me he didn't intend to get soaked every five minutes.'

'What else did he say?'

'He told me about the Minders—they're people who look after things, sometimes in a practical way, sometimes in a caring way.'

'You don't need to worry about Horace Tompkins,' Jim assured Grandfather, 'those tomatoes will grow like nobody else's while he's there. Not that he'll stay indefinitely, of course. He'll move on to other greenhouses, just as I'll move on to other forests.'

'I'm certainly glad to hear that,' said Mr Figge. 'Do you propose taking my logs with you?'

'No, I shall give those to folk who are too poor to buy firewood.'

Mr Figge was quite unable to speak, he was so cross.

'I always give away what's spare,' said Jim.

'These logs *aren't* spare,' shouted Mr Figge, to whom nothing was ever spare. 'And what's more, they aren't yours.'

'Oh, I think they must be spare,' said Jim politely, 'there's such a quantity of old wood lying about; what else is there to do but saw these dead branches into useful logs?'

'If they're Minders,' said Grandfather, 'there's not much we can do. I don't know much about them but I do know they're a very dedicated people and they ignore any opposition to their work.'

'I don't know what you're talking about, Ganderglas,' growled Mr Figge, 'and I haven't heard of these Minders or whatever they're called: but I have heard of trespassers and squatters.'

Minty liked Jim Larchington. She liked his tall, narrow look and the clothes he wore, the colours of a tree, and his long, soft boots that looked like moss.

'Where do you live?' demanded Mr Figge, 'what's your address?'

'At the moment your forest is my address' (Mr Figge stamped his foot in rage) 'but urgent business is taking me back to the Minders' Village as soon as I can get there.'

When Mr Figge heard that Jim Larchington would be leaving, his rage died down a bit and he said gruffly to Grandfather that they'd better get on and look at the rest of the trees. Minty stayed behind. She wanted to ask Jim Larchington about the Minders' Village: she thought he looked as though he'd be more patient about answering questions than Horace Tompkins, and she was quite right. When she asked him if he would tell her about the Village, and about Nathaniel the Clockmaker, he said he'd be delighted.

As things turned out, he wasn't much good at answering

questions, but at least he didn't get impatient. Minty had found that nearly everyone became bored with answering questions very very quickly.

Minty asked first why only Minders could find the Village.

Jim scratched his head.

'No one really knows the answer to that,' he said, 'because there's no reason why anyone shouldn't find the way. But it's a fact that no one does: of course, the Winding Way over the Blue Hills is a very difficult path to follow. Often it disappears and even where it's clearly marked, the twists and turns and double twists are nearly as bad as a maze. People find themselves walking in circles.'

'Do the Minders ever get lost?' asked Minty.

'No, they learn the path from childhood. Minders are the greatest walkers ever. Very young and very old, they think nothing of a day's march and as for the hale and hearty—well!' Jim couldn't express the number of miles they were capable of walking.

'What's the Village like?' asked Minty.

'Quite ordinary.'

'Ordinary?' repeated Minty, very disappointed. 'I thought it was a special sort of place.'

'It *looks* ordinary,' said Jim.

'Then what's special?'

'That's as hard a question to answer as the one about the Winding Way. You see, just as the Winding Way is a perfectly ordinary sort of path, and certainly looks ordinary, after people have been there a little while they are convinced it isn't ordinary at all.'

'Why?' asked Minty. 'What do they feel?'

'That depends on the sort of people they are. Different people feel differently.'

'And Nathaniel?' asked Minty. 'Can you tell me about Nathaniel?'

'Now that's much easier,' said Jim. 'Nathaniel's a very old, very little, very gentle, man who wears suits of thin yellow wool and a dark green cloak and a polka dot hat, and lives in a little stone house with his cat, Fergusson.' He added, in a professional sort of way: 'There's a rather nice plum tree in the garden. I've often seen Nathaniel and Fergusson sitting under it, having their tea. Nathaniel's a bit different from the rest of us. For instance, while I look after forests and Horace Tompkins looks after tomatoes, and Fred Steeple looks after churches, Nathaniel doesn't simply look after clocks, although he does this. He makes clocks as well, marvellous clocks. His chiming clocks have a chime as beautiful as a lark's song, unless they strike the hour loud as a drum; and then there are his weather clocks—'

'What's a weather clock?' asked Minty.

'A weather clock,' Jim explained, 'has two little doors, and when the weather is going to be fine, one of those doors opens and a little girl comes out, carrying a parasol: and when the weather is going to be wet, the other door opens and a little boy comes out, carrying an umbrella.'

'That's a useful clock to have,' said Minty.

'Then there are the cuckoo clocks. When the hour strikes, and the cuckoo's door opens, the cuckoo not only comes out, but flies round the room, calling out what hour it is, and then flies all round the house before returning to its little painted door.'

'My,' breathed Araminta, 'I'd like a clock like that.'

'You'd like his grandfather clocks, too. They have pictures painted on them such as you'll never see anywhere else.'

'What kind of pictures?'

'Peaceful ones. Pictures that give you the same kind of feeling as sitting under a tree on a summer afternoon in a buttercup meadow.'

Just the kind of picture Minty liked.

'And lastly there are the rarest clocks of all, and those are Nathaniel's talking clocks for lonely people. When Nathaniel goes on one of his clock-minding expeditions, he always takes a few of his talking clocks with him; they're quite small, you see, and when he meets a lonely person, he puts a talking clock in their house as a nice surprise.'

'We haven't a clock,' Minty said. 'Aunt Tilly Humble gets up when she hears Mr Figge driving his cows to pasture and we have supper when he drives them back to the farm again; and we have our midday meal somewhere between.'

'That seems a very good arrangement,' said Jim.

Minty thought that a clock would be better, and perhaps Jim thought so, too, because he said:

'When I go to the Village I'll see if Nathaniel has a clock to spare. He probably has, though usually his clocks go only to the lonely and needy.'

'We're not needy,' said Araminta, 'not rich, you know, but not needy. We're caretakers. We're looking after the Old House on the other side of the downs.'

'Caretakers and Minders are almost the same profession,' Jim told her.

'As well as being caretakers,' said Minty, 'Mother is a herbalist, father's a poet and Grandfather Ganderglas is an inventor.' Then she saw Grandfather and Mr Figge, and because she didn't want Mr Figge to start shouting at Jim again, she said goodbye and hurried to meet them. When she looked back, Jim Larchington had disappeared and she saw only trees.

Mr Figge grumbled about Jim and the wood he had sawed into logs all the way up to the track of the old ox drove, and all the way down the chalk path to the lane. He was still grumbling when he stumped off down the lane to the farm, and Minty and Grandfather and Misery turned the other way, towards the Old House.

Minty wished, as they rounded the bend in the lane and saw the gates of the house, that she and Grandfather were returning home: because no one could properly call a house home when they lived there only as caretakers, not even when they loved the house as much as the Humbles did.

Aunt Tilly Humble had baked a honey cake for supper

and boiled five brown eggs. Boiling eggs to the liking of the family, said Tilly, was more difficult than cooking a dozen dinners.

Grandfather Ganderglas liked his boiled hard as a boot. Coriander liked hers softer than Grandfather's but harder than Tilly's. Jan liked his egg to be soft in the yolk, but hard in the white part. Minty didn't mind about the actual boiling so long as she had a brown egg, preferably freckled.

'Did you find any sweet woodruff in the forest?' asked Coriander as they sat down.

'No,' said Grandfather, 'we found a Minder,' and he told them about the logs that Jim had sawn up, and the fury of Farmer Figge. The family laughed heartily. Then Grandfather told them about Horace Tompkins, and how Minty had kept him secret.

'Her upbringing is all wrong,' said Tilly.

'Meeting a Minder is something I'd keep secret for a while, too,' said Coriander.

'H'm,' said Tilly, as she stood up to make more tea, and everyone knew she was thinking that Minty had inherited her secretive ways from the Ganderglas side of the family, and not the Humble side.

While Tilly made more tea, Grandfather lighted the lamp. Minty loved this moment of the day, when the lamp glowed peacefully, and shadows started to darken the corners of the kitchen. This was the time of day when the family told stories, or Grandfather Ganderglas played his accordion. Sometimes Jan would read one of his poems; sometimes Coriander would sing one of the old songs. She had a beautiful voice, had Coriander.

Tonight, the family talked of the Minders.

'These Minders,' said Tilly, 'what manner of folk are they?'

'They're a very old people,' said Jan, 'a special people, with special talents. You'll never find a destructive Minder, that would be against their nature. Whatever they choose to look after prospers under their care. Old Figge should be grateful to have one in his forest; and we should be pleased to have one here. It's a privilege to have a Minder about the place.'

'Of course I can understand that they aren't always welcome,' said Coriander, 'I daresay there are some people who find them a bit priggish and look on them as interfering busybodies. I don't think I'd want anyone looking after my herbs without my leave.'

'Usually they go only where there's been neglect,' Jan said, 'and absence. Places where there are no people to care. Or where there are people who don't care. Besides, people mostly don't notice the Minders before they're gone again.'

'Aye, they don't stay long,' Grandfather said, 'they're a peripatetic people.'

'Goodness, what words,' said Aunt Tilly Humble. 'What might peripatetic people mean, if you please, Grandfather Ganderglas?'

'I think it means walkers,' Grandfather said, 'but I was using it to mean always on the move.'

'Like us,' said Coriander with a sigh.

'Can you do that with words,' asked Minty, 'make them mean what you want to?'

'I do in my poems,' Jan said, 'when I can't find words that are right.'

'Time that child was in bed,' said Tilly.

'We don't know what the time is,' Minty said.

'Time enough,' returned Tilly.

'We ought to have a clock,' persisted Minty.

'Bless me, whatever next? We've always managed without a clock.'

So Minty told them about Nathaniel the Clockmaker, and the marvellous clocks he made, those which chimed like a lark's song and those which talked, and the cuckoos that flew round the house. And when she had finished, the family realized that, after all, a clock was exactly what they did need.

3

Araminta had been dreaming when she saw the little carriage, dreaming away in one of the old stables and at first she thought the carriage was part of the dream.

The family had cleaned only one of the stables. The others were warm and dirty and stuffy and still. Minty wished there were still horses in the stalls, shuffling in the straw and blowing down their noses, as Misery did. Stables without horses look as lonely as houses without people.

She wondered whether there was a Minder of horses, and whether he might give them an old horse no one else wanted.

She had begun imagining how the stable would look, nicely cleaned, with a horse munching his dinner, when she saw the carriage in the darkest, furthest corner; a real carriage, with a faded painting on the side of the dusty coachwork, a little step to climb up by and a fat buttoned pink velvet cushion to sit on. This was when Minty thought the carriage must be a dream, but the carriage was real and, except for a broken shaft, everything that a carriage should be. Best of all, it was small, small enough for O Misery Me to pull along.

Minty thought about the carriage the whole morning, and decided to astonish the family with the news of her discovery when they had their midday meal. But there was another surprise when the family had their meal. Grandfather brought Horace Tompkins to have his dinner with the family. Fortunately, Tilly had made one of her pies.

Everyone was very surprised when Grandfather came in accompanied by Horace Tompkins. Horace was carrying his purple hat and, when he came nearer the table, he bowed.

Grandfather introduced the family and they all stood up, then leaned down to shake Horace by the hand. Jan fetched a cushion for his chair.

'Which part of this pie would you fancy, Mr Tompkins?' enquired Aunt Tilly Humble. 'This corner has duckling, and this one has baked cucumber, and this one a nice little stuffed marrow, and that one a bunch of buttered carrots and in the middle there's a tiny steak and kidney pudding.'

'A few buttered carrots would suit me nicely,' said Horace, 'and may I say I've never seen a pie the like of that one.'

Tilly blushed, and Minty told Horace about meeting Jim Larchington because she knew that, while Tilly loved people to enjoy her amazing pies, she became very embarrassed when they said so.

Horace looked grave when Minty started talking about Jim Larchington. And when she said that he would be returning to the Village on urgent business, Horace shook his head.

'I'm afraid he won't be able to do that,' he said, 'he had an accident late last night. He fell into one of Farmer Figge's deer traps.'

'*Deer traps!*' echoed the family, horrified.

Horace nodded. 'His leg is very bad. He can't possibly walk back to the Minders' Village.'

'I shall have a word with Figge,' said Grandfather. 'I can't call any man my friend who sets traps for animals.'

'I should think not,' said Jan. 'Can't think why you want him for a friend anyway.'

'Or his warty wife,' said Coriander, rather unkindly. Most of us have a wart at one time or another; but Coriander was still offended that Mrs Figge had rejected her wild thyme ointment. She said she would take Jim Larchington her adderstongue for wounds that afternoon. 'Or perhaps Clowns Woundwort would be better; Solomon's Seal is quite widely used, too.'

Horace stood up and bowed in deference to Coriander's knowledge and then the moment seemed to have come for Minty's great news—the moment when she could astonish the family with her discovery. She took a deep breath. The family knew at once that she had something momentous to tell them. They all looked at her with keen expectation and Minty's news came bursting out.

'I've found a simply *marvellous* little carriage in one of the old stables,' she cried, 'small enough for Misery to pull and big enough for us to sit in.' She added, out of consideration for Misery, 'One at a time.'

'A carriage,' echoed Aunt Tilly Humble, 'there'll be some cobwebs in that, I'm thinking.'

No one else gave a thought to the cobwebs. They were tremendously excited by the news.

'If it's in good working order,' said Grandfather, 'Mr Larchington could travel to the Minders' Village in spite of his accident.'

This is just what had occurred to Minty.

The moment the pie was finished and Horace Tompkins had brushed the crumbs from his knees, and said again how that was a pie of which he'd never known the like, they all set off to the stables.

Aunt Tilly Humble never let visitors help with the washing up. The family would have to do that later, with the supper dishes.

The family was entranced by Minty's carriage, and foresaw many outings. Minty thought only of how Jim Larchington could travel to the Minders' Village in spite of his injured leg—and perhaps bring them back one of Nathaniel's clocks. She watched anxiously while Grandfather tested the wheels, and examined the broken shaft, and looked all over the carriage work for weak places. He seemed to take a very long time, but finally he said: 'I can mend this carriage this afternoon; only needs cleaning and oiling and tightening up here and there, and that shaft replacing.'

'Can we go and tell Jim Larchington?' asked Minty 'Now?'

'This instant,' replied Jan and they set off for the forest,

Coriander, Jan and Minty, but not before Coriander had collected all the ointments and potions she needed for Jim's injured leg.

A walk with Coriander and Jan was much slower than a walk with Grandfather Ganderglas. Jan stopped whenever a gap in the hedge, or beween the trees, showed a nice bit of view, and Coriander kept stopping to look at the wild flowers. Coriander knew the names of all the flowers.

Minty, riding O Misery Me, who was slow enough, goodness knows, reached the track of the ox drove long before Coriander and Jan. Minty stopped there, waiting for them. Misery bent her head and ate a few grasses. Grasses of all kinds were blowing in the wind along the ox drove.

When Coriander and Jan came strolling along, Minty pointed down the track and said: 'That's the way to the Minders' Village, isn't it?'

'The start of the way,' said Jan, 'just the start,' and then he exclaimed at the view, and told Coriander and Minty to look over the heads of Mr Figge's trees to the hills.

'Beautiful,' said Coriander, who had no eyes for views, only for plants.

'Marvellous, father,' said Minty, anxious only to find Jim Larchington.

Jan smiled. He knew that only he really saw the view. 'Come on,' he said, 'let's find this Minder of Trees, Araminta Humble.'

Minty laughed, and Misery swung her ears, and down the hill they all went, holding hands and singing.

When they reached the valley path that led to Little Trumpington, Minty had to admit that she had no idea how to find Jim Larchington. No one would have seen him the first time if he hadn't been rolling pine logs.

Coriander said she was sure they would see him before long, and began looking for juniper. Jan sat on a tree stump with a poetry writing look on his face, and Minty began to feel despondent. The forest was too big to make finding anyone easy. She wished that Horace Tompkins had come with them. Minders were probably good at finding other Minders. After a while, when she had given up all hope of finding Jim, and had started collecting fir cones, she saw O Misery Me coming towards her; and who should be sitting on her back but Jim Larchington.

Minty dropped her cones and ran down the slope.

'Hullo,' called Jim 'hope you don't mind my having borrowed your donkey?' He wore a boot on only one leg; the other was wrapped in dock leaves.

'We came here to look for you,' Minty told him. 'Mother has some adderstongue for your leg.'

'How kind,' said Jim, and slid off Misery, on to his good leg, as Coriander and Jan arrived to be introduced.

When he unwound the dock leaves, they were all aghast at the state of his leg.

'Imagine if I had been an animal, helpless to help myself,' said Jim.

They were silent and desolate, thinking of this.

'Grandfather Ganderglas is going to have a word with Mr Figge about setting traps,' said Minty.

'So am I,' said Jim Larchington. He looked very angry. Minty thought that even Mr Figge would be crushed in spirit when both Jim Larchington and Grandfather told him what they thought about him and his traps. She watched while Coriander bandaged Jim's leg. When she had finished, Jim put back the dock leaves to keep the bandages clean.

'You mustn't walk on that leg,' Coriander said, 'you'll have to hop.'

Jim nodded. 'I've been hopping everywhere,' he said, and sighed.

'We've come to tell you about my discovery,' Minty told him.

'A discovery?' said Jim. 'What might that be?'

'Guess.'

'I know,' Jim said, 'you've discovered a forest.'

'Wrong.'

'An eight-bladed knife.'

'An eight-bladed knife?' repeated Minty in astonishment. 'I've never heard of such a thing.'

'A cloak to keep out the rain and wind and snow?'

'No.'

'I give up.'

So she told him about the carriage, and how it was just the right size to be pulled by O Misery Me, and how, if he would like to, he could ride in it to the Minders' Village instead of postponing his visit because of his injured leg. She felt quite worn out when she'd finished saying all that.

'That's an idea,' said Jim, 'that would solve all my problems.'

Minty felt very pleased. She had never solved anyone's problems before.

Then Jim said: 'Would anyone like to come with me? I believe you need a clock? If you came with me, you could choose one for yourselves.'

'Oh, do let's go,' cried Minty. She had never expected that she would be able to visit Nathaniel's little stone house, and see all his clocks and perhaps watch the cuckoo fly round the house before returning to its little painted door.

'If Coriander and Minty and I would be acceptable to the Village,' Jan said, 'we should be honoured to come.'

'Caretakers are always acceptable to Minders,' Jim told him, 'they look on them as kinsmen.'

'But let it be understood,' Coriander said, 'that you ride, at least until your leg is healed, and we walk.'

Jim looked doubtfully at Minty.

'Minty is a very good walker,' said Coriander. She could be very determined, could Coriander.

When Araminta, Jan and Coriander returned to the house, they found Tilly busy scrubbing the old carriage. Already it looked different. Horace Tompkins was looking on.

'Grandfather Ganderglas has gone to Little Trumpington to buy new shafts,' Tilly told them without looking up.

'Can I help you, Tilly?' asked Araminta.

'Yes, child, you can start polishing.'

'Where's the polish, Tilly?'

'By the broken shaft, child; why don't you use your eyes?'

Jan told Tilly about their meeting with Jim Larchington, and how he had suggested they should acompany him; and how they would like to do this if Tilly and Grandfather Ganderglas didn't mind being left alone.

'Mind?' said Tilly. 'Why should we mind? I'll get a hundred jobs done while you're away; and so will Grandfather Ganderglas.'

Instead of being pleased that Tilly didn't mind, Minty felt a little hurt.

'Won't you miss us, Aunt Tilly Humble?' she asked.

'Bless the child, of course I'll miss you all; and so will Grandfather Ganderglas, but we'll both use the time to good advantage. And when you come back, this old house will be so changed with my cleaning and Grandfather's improvements, you won't know it.'

'Oh, dear,' said Coriander, 'I like things the way they are. Don't let Father make too many improvements, Tilly.'

Aunt Tilly Humble threw up her hands and declared there had never been such contrary folk as her family: never, never, never.

Grandfather not only fixed new shafts to the carriage; he arranged a folding roof that could be pulled up for rain and folded back for sun.

Tilly beat the dust out of the pink velvet cushion. Then she told Minty to fetch the rest of the family to discuss a list she'd made of essentials for the journey.

When Tilly said she had made a list of essentials, what she meant was that she had thought out such a list; and what she wanted to do was to call out all the items so that Jan could write them down. As Tilly often said: put a

duster in her hand, or give her the ingredients for a pie and she knew instantly how to use them; give her a paper and pencil and she was lost. 'And that,' she would say to Minty, 'is because I never had regular lessons.'

'Now,' said Tilly, when everyone was seated round the kitchen table, and Jan had his paper and pencil ready, 'food first. Are you ready to write down what I say, Jan Humble?'

'Quite ready, Tilly.'

'Six pies that can be eaten cold, special pies that last for months. So don't be afraid to bring them back again. But I judge you'll need two for the outward hourney, two for the homeward and two for your stay in the Village. Write that down, too, Jan Humble, or you'll be gobbling them up at the wrong times. Then put fruit and nuts, cake and chocolate, tea, and my long-lasting soup that you can heat over your camp fire; hard-boiled eggs, honey and dates and a bottle of rice and raisin wine in case you become chilled . . .'

'Not so fast,' cried Jan, writing for all he was worth.

'Don't forget my special folding tents, that fold right down to pocket size,' said Grandfather Ganderglas.

'Get those down, Jan Humble,' said Tilly, 'and a change of clothing and . . .'

Jan threw down his pencil. 'There won't be room in the carriage for Jim Larchington if we take any more.'

And there was nothing to be said to that.

'Sure you'll be all right by yourselves, you and Grandfather Ganderglas?' Coriander asked Tilly. Coriander, Jan and Minty had said this more than a dozen times each. Both Grandfather Ganderglas and Aunt Tilly Humble looked thoroughly exasperated when they heard the question yet again, and so did Horace Tompkins. Horace Tompkins could look exasperated very quickly, Minty had noticed.

'They will have *me* here,' he said, 'I shouldn't dream of moving on until you return.'

'There would be far more hazard, my girl,' said Grandfather Ganderglas 'If you and Jan stayed here while Tilly and I accompanied Minty and Jim Larchington. You, Coriander, would never in a thousand years of dusting get round half this great house, and as for what Jan would do if the rain started coming through the roof, or a window blew out or the well ran dry, I do not know.'

Neither did Jan. He looked pale at the thought of such calamities.

'We still need a proper carriage harness for Misery,' Coriander said.

'I purchased one only this afternoon,' said Grandfather.

'*Purchased* one?' echoed Coriander. 'What with?'

'With my savings, girl; I've said before, and I expect I shall have to say again—where would you all be without my savings?'

No one knew. So they all went to the stables to admire the new harness.

That night Minty said goodbye to the house. With her lamp in her hand, she walked down all the corridors and into all the rooms, even those which had dust sheets over the furniture. She longed to see the Village, but she hated to leave the house. The Humbles loved the house more and more: the thought they would have to leave when the caretaking job finished filled them all with unbearable sadness.

4

Coriander and Jan always travelled light, Coriander with her herbs, Jan with his pencils and paper. Grandfather Ganderglas and Aunt Tilly Humble were the ones for packages and bundles and last minute We Might Need This and Thats. Jan had to stand beside the carriage to stop Tilly filling every inch.

When the stores and spare clothing and folding tents were packed in, there was just enough room for one passenger to sit comfortably.

Minty, who was to ride until they met Jim Larchington on the ox drove, climbed aboard.

Grandfather Ganderglas, Tilly and Horace Tompkins shook the travellers by the hand.

'You do know our route, don't you?' said Jan, not for the first time.

Grandfather replied patiently: 'Follow the chalk path up to the downs to the point where it crosses the track of the ancient ox drove; follow the ox drove as far as the Hilltop Town. From the Hilltop Town, you see the Empty Plain, and at the far edge of the Empty Plain, where the blue hills begin to rise, you see the signpost point along the Winding Way to the Minders' Village.'

'You keep forgetting,' said Horace Tompkins, 'that I shall be here. Any assistance that may be required, *I* can give.'

'Have you taken herbs, Coriander,' asked Tilly, 'to cover dangers and difficulties you may meet on the way?'

'I've taken adderstongue and wild prunella for injury; briony for vertigo; knotted figwort for boils; camomile to stop earache, pursloe should we suffer from bad dreams, and borage in case we feel melancholy.'

'I thought you were reckoning on enjoying yourselves,' said Grandfather Ganderglas.

'Time they went,' said Aunt Tilly Humble.

So the magic moment had come when O Misery Me took her first step forward, and the wheels of the carriage turned, and everyone cheered.

Tilly, Grandfather and Horace walked with the travellers as far as the gate, and stood there, waving goodbye as Misery clattered into the lane. Coriander, Jan and Minty kept turning to wave, while Misery walked steadily on, into patches of sunlight and then through the shadow of the trees that grew from the deep green banks. And then the lane curved, and the travellers could no longer see Grandfather and Tilly and Horace Tompkins, standing and waving by the gates of the Old House. Now they were really on their way.

When they reached the opening to the chalk path, Minty jumped out of the carriage so that Misery had less weight to pull uphill.

They hadn't gone far up the track, the carriage bumping over the ruts and stones, brushed by ferns and cow parsley, when they heard a loud barking; and there was Wag, waving his plumy tail and smiling.

'You can't come with us, old son,' said Jan. Wag raced on ahead and disappeared. They didn't have another glimpse of him until they reached the ox drove, and there he was again sitting with Jim Larchington.

Jim had a small bundle beside him, wrapped in moss, and two pine sticks which he must have used as crutches.

'That dog belongs to Figge,' Jan told him.

Jim Larchington laughed. He thought Wag very sensible in wanting to travel to the Minders' Village rather than live with Mr Figge. So no more was said, and when Jim was settled in the carriage, and Misery had eaten a few grasses and was ready to start again, Wag took it on himself to look after them all, now hurrying along in front, now following at the back. He was a bit of a Minder too, Minty thought.

The sun was still shining, but the wind was blowing, too, and the wind blew cold and strong up there on the old ox drove that had once been a prehistoric highway and trading route; or so it was believed. In those earliest days, people had lived in hilltop settlements for safety and there were still traces to be found of the first villages in the land.

Jan told Minty about those early days as they walked along, about forgotten people, early battles and vanished customs; about the legends that still persisted.

The ox drove was a track that changed as the miles followed one another: sometimes it was stony and bare, sometimes grassy, enclosed by hedges. Hedges that were truly wild, bursting with elder and fern, holly and oak, with sloe and spindle, honeysuckle and wild roses.

Some people thought autumn the best time to walk the ox drove, when the spindle waxed orange, lighting up miles of the track as though by fire, and some said June, when the wild roses hung in great pink fronds; now, as April hurried into May, there was honeysuckle in the hedges and tiny orchids among the grass and buttercups that looked like melting gold.

Jim Larchington sat in the carriage very reluctantly. He kept on and on about how embarrassed he felt to be riding while everyone else walked. He might just as well have sat quietly and enjoyed the passing scene because the family didn't even hear.

Coriander was on the lookout for herbs. Coriander said she had found some of her best plants in hedgerows and woods. Grandfather Ganderglas had told her to be careful not to find any in Mr Figge's woods: fortunately, there was no need to worry about Mr Figge on the Ox Drove. No need to worry about anyone on that lonely track. Not that Coriander worried much anyway; especially when she was looking for plants. She walked in a very abstracted fashion, staring down at the thick hedgerow grass and murmuring little reminders to herself, such as 'Camomile for hysteria and headache, white horehound for coughs and colds, juniper for the kidneys.'

Jan was just the opposite. Far from staring at the ground all the time, Jan walked with his eyes on the clouds (and his head in them, Aunt Tilly Humble would have said, had she been there). The clouds were fat and fleecy and white, big as mountains in the blue sky. They had shadows, too, blown across the downs by the wind. The clouds above and the shadows below seemed to join the sky and the earth together.

As for Minty, she tried to look everywhere at once: at the flowers and the clouds and the carriage that trundled along behind Misery and the track that wound ahead, on and on and on.

Two hours later they stopped for a piece of pie. Jim was open-mouthed at the size of the pie.

Tilly had dictated labels to Jan, describing the contents of the six pies and these had been stuck to each one with a skewer.

When everyone was sitting down, leaning against a bank of grasses, out of the wind and facing a fine view, Coriander read out the label describing the contents of the pie they had chosen.

In one corner there was pheasant and watercress, in another a mushroom salad, in the third, a ham pancake, in the fourth a little cauliflower in a cheese sauce and in the middle a few potatoes flavoured with oranges and covered by nuts.

Minty always thought food tasted better eaten outside, even pie. Now that she was sitting down, she felt tired, but nicely tired, the sort of tired that a rest among grasses and buttercups and daisies instantly banishes.

'I do like buttercups,' said Minty.

'You mustn't just say "buttercups",' Coriander told her, 'there are different kinds of buttercup: creeping buttercups, and bulbous buttercups, and small flowered buttercups and pale hairy buttercups and corn buttercups.'

'I'll hop along for a while this afternoon,' said Jim. 'I can do so quite nicely with these sticks of mine; and Minty must ride. She's walked far enough.'

The family argued about this all the time they ate their pie, but they wasted their breath. It's no use arguing with a Minder. When they set off again, Minty sat in the carriage, and Jim fixed his pine crutches under his arms and hopped alongside.

They didn't meet a single person, not one. Rabbits and hares scampered ahead of them; and occasional squirrel raced along the branches of a tree, and sometimes the bright, wicked eyes of a weasel gleamed from the hedgerow. Birds, startled by the sound of voices and the rumble of carriage wheels, flew up from the woods, and Wag pretended to chase them.

There were deer, too, swift and beautiful, and Minty saw a sparrow-hawk high overhead, still as a stone, waiting to drop on its prey. They must have eyes like telescopes, those sparrowhawks, Minty thought.

On either side of the track, the land had been planted with corn. Here and there Minty saw an early poppy.

'I do love poppies,' she said, 'they're so cheerful.'

'You mustn't just say "poppies",' Coriander told her, 'there are different kinds of poppy, the Common Red Poppy, the Long Smooth-headed Poppy, the Long Rough-

Headed Poppy, the Opium Poppy, the Yellow Haired Poppy and the Violet Haired Poppy.'

When the afternoon turned to evening, and the hollows filled with mist, Jim Larchington said it was time to stop and light a fire. And put up the tents, said Jan.

Jim looked surprised. Where could the tents be? No one was carrying a bundle. When Minty showed him how small they folded, and how they were lying unnoticed on the floor of the carriage, he was amazed. Those tents, he said, were an invention the Minders could do with. They were always being caught out by the weather on their travels.

Jim Larchington and Jan put up the four tents while Minty collected wood to make a fire, and large stones to make a fireplace. Wag helped her. Or thought he was helping. Coriander sorted out the pie, which had become jumbled during the afternoon.

Grandfather's tents went up as easily as toadstools and when Jan had lighted the fire, inside the circle of stones, that high, lonely spot looked quite snug.

Minty saw other lights while she watched the flames grow, lights that looked a long way off. Had they not been steady, steadfast as tiny beacons, Minty might have thought them Will o' the Wisp lights. When she pointed them out to Jim, he told her they were the lights of the Hilltop Town. Minty wondered whether the people of the Hilltop Town would be able to see their fire up on the Ox Drove and what they would think if they could. 'Look at that light up there on the old Ox Drove,' they might say. 'Whatever can be happening?' And because they couldn't guess and didn't like mysteries, they would probably draw their curtains and cook their suppers and count themselves lucky to live safe and cosy between neighbours.

Coriander laid out pie and fruit. Jim fed the animals.

Jan opened a bottle of rice and raisin wine to warm them all up, and Minty watched more lights come on in the Hilltop Town. Then she ate her pie while the fire grew warm and the sky grew dark and she grew very sleepy. Her thoughts sank into confusion, and this was a pity because Jan read out his poem and Jim Larchington said he had the heart of a Minder and Minty missed most of what was said. But she heard enough of Jan's poem to know she had been wrong to think that 'caring' was a funny subject.

Jan had written about the need everyone has to help as well as to be helped, to look after as well as to be looked after; to care. Jan's poem made you feel as well as to understand the importance of caring. Minty knew that understanding is no use unless you feel what you learn to be true.

After this the fire seemed to become very bright but rather cold, and Minty blinked and shivered; and realized that the brightness was the sun shining and that morning was all round her. Somehow, she had slept through the night in her tent without even noticing that Jan had carried her from the side of the fire.

The evening felt a dream now, their whole journey felt a dream, but the morning was real enough and, when she looked outside her tent, she saw the ashes of the fire inside the ring of stones. And there, away in the distance, where the night before she had seen the lights of the Hilltop Town, was the town itself, a dark patch of buildings in the pink mist of morning.

Minty stepped outside her tent and Wag woke up and came to greet her. He had been sleeping just inside Jim Larchington's tent and within a few minutes Jim looked out, too; and then Jan looked out of his tent, and

Coriander out of hers, yawning and saying she could sleep for a month.

Jim lit a new fire in the ashes of the old, so that Coriander could heat water to make tea. Several cups of hot, strong tea was the way the Humbles always started the day.

Jan examined Misery's legs and feet to make sure she hadn't suffered through pulling the carriage so far; Misery sniffed the air for breakfast.

After breakfast, Jan fitted Misery's harness, and Coriander put new bandages on Jim's leg. She told him the wound was nearly healed, but that he must ride at least as far as the Hilltop Town. That, she said, had been the understanding when they came. She spoke quite severely. Coriander could become very stern over medical matters.

They reached the Hilltop Town just before midday. The

town was quite small, and built of grey stone with streets so steep and so narrow that people could look from the windows of the houses on one side straight through the windows on the other side and into the rooms.

There were shops in the Hilltop Town, and a market, and the ruins of a castle; the castle wall was still standing, and the travellers leaned their backs against the rough stones while they stared down on the Empty Plain.

Minty had never seen so vast a space. The sheep that grazed there looked small as pins and the few scattered homesteads as lonely as a handful of stars.

There were dark ridges, where trees bent to the winds that swept that great empty space, and white ribbons where paths had been cut in the chalk. And in the centre of the Empty Plain, with a spire that rose as high as thought, they saw a mighty church. And then the wind blew the clouds away from the sun and all the plain was polished in colours that were as pale as they were bright and as for the church—Minty had never seen anything so beautiful as the sun shining on that mighty church in the vast space of the Empty Plain.

'Fred Steeple's favourite church,' Jim told them, 'you'll always find Fred in that church. He shouldn't be, of course, because that church is one of the best cared for in the land, and the duty of the Minders is towards the neglected. There's strong feeling in the Village about Fred Steeple always finding excuses to visit the great church on the Empty Plain.'

'Who can be the people who care for such a lonely church?' asked Minty.

'People travel to that church from near and far, from all over the world,' Jim said. 'Compared with that church, the

Minders' Village has no fame at all, is just a speck on the map.'

He spoke so fervently that Minty knew he must love the great church, too.

'Come on,' he said, 'Let's visit Fred.'

Jan kept a hand on the front of the carriage as they went down the steep road to the Empty Plain, for fear it should topple on to Misery, and Coriander held the back. Minty walked in front of Misery and Wag pranced along in front of Minty.

They were a long time reaching the church. They seemed to walk towards it all the morning without getting nearer, and then suddenly the church towered in front of them and they stood marvelling at that rare building, so massive and yet so delicate.

Jan told Wag to keep Misery company while they went inside to find Fred Steeple.

When Minty followed Jim into the church, she understood why Fred Steeple had to keep returning there: not for the grandeur of the immense nave or lofty roof, not even because of the great silver cross or the carved choir stalls or the tiny chapels folded secretly away. No doubt Fred cherished all these, but what was most striking of all was the feeling inside that church. Minty would never have believed that a place so awe-inspiring from the outside could feel so gentle and holy and homely inside.

They searched for Fred for a long time before they discovered him polishing the corner of a stained glass window. And then they might not have seen him had he not been sitting on a ledge with his legs dangling down; because the corner of the window he was polishing was deep crimson, the exact colour of Fred Steeple's jersey.

'Hullo there, Fred,' called Jim Larchington.

Fred peered down: and here was something else Minty was to learn about the Minders—just as Horace Tompkins had the look of a tomato, and Jim Larchington the look of a tree, so had Fred Steeple the look of a church.

He was taller than either Horace or Jim, and Jim told Minty later that the Steeples were the tallest of all Minders. Tall and thin was Fred Steeple, with a face that might have been carved from a piece of stone. Minty had never seen such a flinty, granite-like face. But cheerful. When Fred Steeple smiled, and he smiled the moment he saw them, and started to climb down from the ledge, that stony face cracked into a thousand pieces. When he stopped smiling, the cracks all closed up again.

'Have you had an accident?' he asked Jim, when he saw the crutches, and Jim told him about the deer trap. Then he introduced the Humbles '—Coriander Humble, a herbalist and Jan Humble, a poet, and their daughter, Araminta: all three of them caretakers.'

'Minders and Caretakers are kinsmen,' Fred Steeple said, as Jim had done, his face cracking again into a smile. 'Come to the cloisters, and share my lunch.'

'We'll come to the cloisters,' Coriander said, 'but we would like you to share our lunch.'

Jan held up a string bag that was bulging with the second of Tilly's pies.

'My, what a pie,' exclaimed Fred Steeple, 'what can be inside a pie that size?'

Jan read out the label: 'Artichoke hearts on the west side of this pie; beans and black pudding on the east; a Burgundian Cheese Loaf to the north, waffles to the south and a few Alsatian Noodles in the middle.'

'My!' said Fred again.

By now they had reached the cloisters.

'Ever seen cloisters the like of these?' demanded Fred, as proud as though those cloisters were his.

Minty looked at the open sided stone passages that joined in a square. There were stone arches along the sides of this square and the arches were finished with stone circles; within each circle there was a carved flower. The stone masons must have had a wild time when they fashioned those cloisters.

'I should want to keep coming back to this church, too,' Minty whispered to Fred.

'There!' cried Fred. 'One visit, and the little lass wants to come back. So how should I not wish to come again and again, knowing as I do every stone and every rafter, every step of the stair that winds to the library, every pane of stained glass window?'

'Because this church doesn't need you, Fred,' Jim said sternly, 'and there are others that do.'

Fred ignored him.

'I wish,' he said, 'I could have been here seven hundred years ago, at the time of building. Imagine, just imagine, seeing this great church rise, imagine having a part in *that!* Think of the excitement, the comings and goings of stonemasons and carpenters; think of being infected by the spirit that infected them. Whole summers and winters passing. Thirty-eight years they took to build this church, I'm told. A man could have started as an apprentice here and been nearing the end of his working life as the last stone was laid.' Fred's face glowed and shone at the thought. 'Have you ever been told,' he asked Minty, 'of the stonemason who was working on one of these great churches, and someone saw him chipping out his finished work from a dark corner? He said he'd made a bungle of that corner and when he was told that no one would know, he said that he'd know so he must put the corner right. I can understand exactly what that stonemason meant.'

'That's all very well, Fred,' interrupted Jim, who had heard this story from Fred Steeple many times before, 'but there are other churches, neglected churches: no one can call this church neglected.'

'Still needs watching,' said Fred, his tone obstinate, 'beetle might get into the woodwork, or rust into the organ, or moth into the hassocks. So—' and here he fixed Jim Larchington with a stony gaze—'I've decided to stay here for good.' And he ate at a large mouthful of pie.

'Stay for good!' echoed Jim. '*Stay for good*! You can't, Fred. Minders can't be choosers. Supposing I took a fancy to a particular forest and refused to visit any other?'

'I'd say good luck to you,' said Fred.

'Now look here, Fred—'

'No use carrying on,' said Fred, 'my mind's made up. I fret when I'm away from this church. There are other Steeples, after all, dozens of them. There are more Steeple Minders than any other kind. If they do their work diligently, they can look after all the neglected churches. Take the High-Steeples: there are seventy-five High-Steeples, including the second cousins, and every one of them active. Then take the Low Steeples—there were *one hundred and twenty-five* Low-Steeples at the last count, not including the pensioners, and they are perfectly good for watching jobs.'

'There'll be trouble in the Village even so, over this decision of yours,' said Jim. 'There's principle at stake.'

'There's trouble of a worse kind that will take folks' minds off me,' said Fred. 'Albert Carpenter and Sidney Berry are trying to steal Nathaniel's clocks.'

Minty gasped and Jim looked grave at the news.

'I'd heard rumours that they were trying to reach the Village; I was told by a woodcutter who had the tale from the Figges' dairymaid who'd been selling Figge eggs in the Hilltop Town. But no one knew what they were after. That's why I wanted to return to the Village. I wanted to warn everyone that Albert and Sidney were on the prowl.'

'Well, you're too late for that,' said Fred, 'but I expect they'll be pleased to have you there. Albert and Sidney don't give up easily, and they'll probably have another try.'

'Who are Albert Carpenter and Sidney Berry?' asked Jan. they'd brew trouble as far as the crow flies.'

'Burglars,' replied Jim. 'Villains through and through. All the trouble that's brewed hereabouts is brewed by Albert Carpenter and Sidney Berry; and if they weren't so lazy,

'What do they look like?' asked Minty, who had never knowingly met a burglar.

'Some might call their clothes modish,' said Fred, 'I call them flashy.'

Jim nodded in agreement with this.

'Inconsiderate manners,' continued Fred, 'and harsh voices.'

Minty felt a little sorry for Albert and Sidney, having so many disadvantages.

'I'm told,' said Fred, who was told a lot on account of the numbers of people who visited the great church on the Empty Plain, 'I'm told Albert and Sidney have had their greedy eyes on Nathaniel's clocks for a long time. They know they're worth a mint of money. They're unique, those clocks. If Nathaniel sold them, he'd be a rich man.'

'Then he'd have to stop being a Minder,' said Jim. 'There are no rich Minders.'

'Albert and Sidney knew they would never reach the Village by themselves,' continued Fred, 'but they thought that they might be able to if they followed closely enough behind Nathaniel. And this is what they tried to do. When Nathaniel visited the Hilltop Town, they waited and followed him. Nathaniel hadn't noticed them loitering about the Hilltop Town, and he didn't notice them behind him as he walked home . . .'

'What a long walk at each end of the day,' remarked Coriander.

'Minders never notice the length of a walk, not even old Minders,' Jim told her. 'Walking's in a Minder's blood. Stop a Minder walking or minding, and he's finished.' He turned to Fred. 'What happened as Albert and Sidney followed Nathaniel?'

'At first they seemed to be succeeding in their plan to

reach the Village, and I daresay they were feeling very pleased with themselves, when suddenly the path took a turn and Nathaniel vanished. That's what happens: Albert and Sidney raced round the corner, but they couldn't see Nathaniel, and when they did see him again he was miles and miles ahead of them. So they walked very quickly to catch up. They walked faster and faster and Nathaniel walked more and more slowly, but the distance between them grew and grew. So Albert and Sidney started to run, and they're very speedy runners, but they were soon lost in the whirls and twists of the path and Nathaniel was out of sight. So Albert and Sidney mooched back to the Hilltop Town, very cross and disgruntled. But they didn't give up. The next time Nathaniel went to town, they were seen talking to him. I suppose they thought that if they actually walked with him, they'd be bound to reach the Village; and that's just where they were wrong. At first the plan seemed to work quite well, as the other one had. They'd gone a long way towards the Village with Nathaniel when suddenly they walked into a patch of mist. The path was sunny in front and sunny behind, but the part on which they were walking was so densely misty that Sidney and Albert couldn't see one another. They couldn't see their own feet. They had to stand still. Nathaniel walked on without realizing he'd left them behind, and when they had shuffled out of the mist and stood in sunshine again, they were very angry to discover that they had walked backwards and Nathaniel was out of sight.'

'And has Nathaniel been warned by all this to take extra care?' asked Jim.

'Bless you no,' said Fred Steeple, 'Nathaniel would never believe anyone meant to rob him.'

'Well, I expect the rest of the Village is on the alert,'

remarked Jim, 'but Albert and Sidney won't give up yet and they have very cunning ways. We'd best get on.'

Fred came with them to the door of the church, and stood in the porch waving goodbye, as Jim climbed into the carriage after the usual argument, and Jan turned Misery's head, and Wag started leaping about because he was always excited when they started off again.

Minty kept turning round to wave back to Fred; and each time she turned she thought how this must be the most beautiful church in the land, so magnificent, so gentle and so serene.

5

The atmosphere of their journey changed as they set off towards the Blue Mountains. Now there was threat in the air. No one felt happy-go-lucky any more. Even Wag stayed close to the carriage, his eyes wary and his ears pricked for trouble.

'Just mention the names of Albert Carpenter and Sidney Berry,' Jim told them, 'and everyone's spirits drop to their boots. Some folk bring happiness with them, and some bring peace, and some bring good fortune and some excitement and some, argument. Albert and Sidney bring gloom and despondency. They bring destruction.' Jim sounded grim. Destruction is the opposite of all a Minder's ideals, the reverse of their whole purpose in life.

Jim brooded on the mischief Albert and Sidney might be plotting all the way across the Empty Plain towards the Blue Hills.

Jan was looking gloomy, too. Minty wondered whether he was wishing he hadn't read out his poem the night before. Jan always said that he felt a poem stopped belonging to him once he read it out. So long as a poem remained unknown to anyone, he could go on working, altering a line here and a word there: but once he had read out his poem that was that, and he lost interest.

Coriander was the most cheerful because she had found a nice little root of Viper's Bugloss which, she told everyone, was an excellent remedy against poisonous bites and poisonous herbs.

This news didn't cheer anyone. Jan said he hadn't known there were any poisonous herbs and he only hoped Aunt Tilly Humble had been careful about those she had put in the pies.

Coriander told him not to be silly. He knew very well that she, Coriander Humble, who had been Coriander Ganderglas of a long line of herbalists, supplied Tilly with all the herbs she needed.

They took the whole afternoon to travel to the hills. Misery walked slowly, just when they would have liked to travel fast, and the wind held them back, too.

They had thought the wind cold up there on the Ox Drove, but down on the Empty Plain there was a wind fierce enough to blow you inside out because there were so few trees or hedges. Nothing stopped the wind there. But Minty liked the Plain. The sun swept that space as well as the wind; larks soared and sang in the endless sky and, when Minty turned to look over her shoulder, she saw the spire of the great church. She never forgot the sound of the larks or the glimpses of the spire. Never. Not even when she was a grandmother.

'Look,' Jim said, 'there's the signpost pointing to the Minders' Village.'

Minty looked beyond the signpost. 'Is that really the Winding Way?' she asked. 'That narrow little path?'

Jim nodded. 'Gets narrower,' he said, 'and sometimes disappears altogether.'

'My,' whispered Minty, and hoped there would be room for the carriage on that narrow, twisting track.

Jim suggested they should camp by the signpost, and set

off on the last part of their journey in the morning. This would give O Misery Me a good long rest.

'Shall I collect wood for a fire?' Minty asked.

'Yes,' said Coriander, 'some hot tea will warm us, and a glassful of my syrup of borage might be a good idea—I've never seen such long faces. I knew I was right to bring borage. No one knows when melancholia may strike.'

While Coriander unpacked their supper, Jan and Jim put up the tents: then Jim lit a fire with the wood that Minty had been collecting.

There was a lot of wood lying about, but very few stones. Jim said over and over again how necessary it was to make a fire within a good ring of stones for safety's sake.

This camp felt quite different from their last one—perhaps because they were on flat land instead of being high on the ridgeway. Tonight, the distant lights of the Hilltop Town shone above them. The great church was far away, too, but Minty could still see the spire, frail as a thread in the darkening sky. She wondered what Fred Steeple was doing: whether he had finished polishing the window and what he would have for supper, and where he found his food, and whether he slept inside or outside the church. There was a lot she would like to ask Fred Steeple.

Now the fire was really burning. Sparks were jumping and cracking from the wood. Jim Larchington was a great hand at starting a fire. Soon it was hot enough to boil their kettle. Everyone sat close to the blaze. Their faces grew red as Horace Tompkins' cheeks. Misery and Wag were there, too, close together. With everyone crowded near the warmth, there wasn't an inch of space round that fire. They all felt much happier. The threat of Albert and Sidney faded in the warmth and companionship. Coriander sang them a song, and they were all so busy joining in the chorus,

and drinking tea, and sipping borage syrup, that no one noticed the stranger approach and stand there, behind the bright circle of the fire. He stood listening and watching for a long time before Jim Larchington suddenly looked up. On seeing the stranger he drew a sharp breath and cried out in his most forbidding voice: 'And who may you be, my good sir?'

The stranger was tall, and his face had been coloured by sun and wind and rain: perhaps by frost as well. His boots were stout, the boots of a walker, and much worn. Those boots looked as though they'd tramped a mile or two.

A shabby cloak hung from his shoulders, and he carried a pack. A pedlar, perhaps, or a tramp; and yet, as they looked at him, standing there so tall and silent in the shadows of the fire, he seemed to have an authority and a freedom that suggested he had chosen poverty for himself. He had a mysterious look, that man.

'Who are you, sir?' asked Jim once more.

The man, when he replied, spoke slowly, and his voice was deep.

'You may as well call me Wayfarer since my business takes me all over.'

'What business?' demanded Jim, 'and what do you mean by "all over"?'

'Just so that we can all introduce ourselves,' said Jan, as though hoping to soften Jim's sharp words.

Minty had noticed that both Horace Tompkins and Jim could be very sharply spoken. Not Fred. He seemed obstinate, did Fred, but not sharp.

Wayfarer didn't seem at all put out by Jim's unfriendly manner.

'Paths and rights of way are my business. I keep them open. There are farmers and landowners who forget that many tracks belong to the people as of ancient right. Either forget or don't want to remember. They put up notices with "Keep Out" or they plough up paths when they plough the land, and gradually people forget the paths were ever there.'

'What do you do, to keep these paths open?' asked Jim.

'If a wire fence is blocking a path, I call on the farmer and tell him that if he won't move the fence, there are official ways of restoring the paths to the people.'

'Solicitors?' asked Minty.

'Solicitors might come into the matter,' Wayfarer agreed, 'but I always hope to manage without them.'

'Grandfather would agree with you,' said Minty.

'What else do you do?' asked Jim.

'If there are notices saying "Keep Out", I put up other

notices, reminding people of their rights. Often, though, the tracks are simply overgrown with bramble and nettle and then all I have to do is to clear them.'

'Shouldn't think you've had much clearing to do on your walk across the Plain,' said Jan.

'No,' agreed Wayfarer, looking back towards the Empty Plain, 'there's no clearing to be done on the tracks across the Plain. Nowhere can people walk in such space; nowhere is there such short springy grass to walk on, or such air to breathe. All four winds of heaven blow across the Empty Plain: the north carries the smell of snow and the west the freshness of rain, and the south carries the scent of all the flowers and grasses. The east—' Wayfarer paused, as though remembering what he'd suffered from the east wind over the years. 'I could do without the east,' he admitted, 'but there's no place like the Plain.' Then he opened his pack, showing them his bundles of maps, maps that covered the land for fifty miles north, south, east and west of the great church.

No wonder Wayfarer's boots were shabby, Minty thought. Some of the maps were very old and some quite new. Some had been drawn with two and a half inches to the mile. These showed every detail of the landscape. They showed churches and farms and bridges and woods and even stiles and gates. Other maps covered whole counties, showing only rivers and towns and land that was flat and land that was high.

The maps which Wayfarer had drawn himself were confined to the tracks and paths that he had cleared through woodland, and followed over hillsides, and established along river banks and across fields. These were paths that belonged to everyone and, if Wayfarer succeeded in his work, would always do so.

Wayfarer explained his maps very carefully, pointing out paths that had been there from the earliest days, paths he had cleared, paths he had restored, and paths that farmers and landowners pretended weren't there and Wayfarer insisted were there. These paths were coloured red because Wayfarer had to keep checking on them.

All the names, whether of towns, villages or hamlets, were printed in the most beautiful script Minty had ever seen, and she asked Jan if he would teach her to print like that. Jan replied that he had never been taught such marvellous script and only wished he had.

By now Jim was looking at Wayfarer in a more friendly way.

'Your work is quite acceptable,' he said, 'really very similar to that of myself and my fellows.'

'Jim's a Minder,' Minty told Wayfarer.

'I know,' said Wayfarer, 'I had been told.'

'Where do you live?' asked Coriander.

'Where my work takes me. I sleep in the nearest shelter—under hedges, in barns. Anywhere.'

'You mean you've no home?' asked Minty, feeling sad for this lonely man. Even Minders who 'lived on the job,' as Horace Tompkins put it, had the Village to go home to.

Wayfarer hesitated. 'I do have a home, I suppose, but I'm never there because my work takes me in so many different directions. I never have time.'

'We have time,' said Jan, laughing, 'but no home. We're caretakers. We spend our time in other people's houses.'

'I know,' said Wayfarer again.

'I suppose you've learned about us by visiting the great church and talking with Fred Steeple,' asked Jim. 'Fred's gossiping and indiscretions know no bounds.'

'I have been to the great church,' Wayfarer replied, 'and I

I did speak with Fred, but only to find out how far ahead of me you were. I knew that if you'd reached the Blue Hills and started on your journey along the Winding Way, I wouldn't be able to find you, but that if you were still on the Empty Plain I should have no difficulty.'

'You were only just in time,' said Minty, and Wayfarer nodded.

'If Fred didn't tell you about us and our journey, who did?' demanded Jim.

'I was told when I called at the Old House,' Wayfarer told them, and looked quietly pleased at the astonishment on their faces.

'I hope you haven't opened a right of way through my herb garden?' asked Coriander.

'Why not?' said Jan. 'Think how nice for people to walk through your herb garden.'

'Nice for them,' said Coriander.

'I stopped to admire your herb garden,' Wayfarer told her, 'but not to make a right of way there. The rights of way I was anxious about were those through Farmer Figge's forest. I wanted to make sure he hadn't closed the ones I re-opened a couple of years ago.'

'I expect he had,' said Jan.

'I see you know Farmer Figge. He's the worst man I know for closing paths and driving people out. I found notices and wire and even a barricade of branches across my paths.' Wayfarer glanced at Wag. 'Now he's saying you've stolen his dog.'

Wag waved his tail, but Jan looked anxious.

'We couldn't stop Wag coming,' said Coriander.

'Oh, don't worry about Figge,' said Wayfarer, 'I don't. He's in a particular rage at the moment because your

Grandfather Ganderglas has made him move all his deer traps. I wish I knew how.'

'Father can be very forceful,' said Coriander.

'Were he and Tilly and Horace Tompkins well?' asked Jan.

'In excellent health, all three. I was given many messages to pass on to you of goodwill and come back soon, but not to think they aren't managing splendidly.'

'Why did you go to the Old House when your business was with Farmer Figge?' Jim asked, and Minty hoped he wasn't becoming suspicious again.

'I always call there when I visit Figge's forest because I love that house.'

'So do we,' said Araminta, 'we've never taken care of a house we love so well.'

'That house is all anyone needs in a house,' said Coriander.

'Rather more than most people need,' said Jan, 'it's the kind of house people dream about rather than live in.'

'Have you been looking for us just to give us the messages of goodwill?' asked Coriander.

'No,' said Wayfarer, 'I also have a message for Mr Larchington from Horace Tompkins.'

'Why not sit down first,' suggested Jan, 'and warm your hands at the fire and have some supper.'

So Wayfarer sat down and Coriander cut him a piece of pie, and Jan opened the second bottle of rice and raisin wine to celebrate a new friendship. And then Wayfarer passed on Horace Tompkins' message which was that Albert Carpenter and Sidney Berry had been joined by the Youth. Jim gave a loud cry of dismay when he heard this.

'What youth?' asked Coriander. 'What's his name?'

'He's only ever called the Youth,' said Jim, 'he's the one

black shadow in the history of the Minders. We've had lazy Minders, and Minders, like Fred, who insist on looking after something dear to their hearts, but the Youth's a rebel and a renegade; the Youth can't stand minding. The Youth jeers at our ideals. The Youth's a traitor and a a materialist.' Jim didn't mince matters over the Youth. 'He comes from good stock, too. His family has minded rivers and streams and dew ponds for generations. Not the ocean, of course—that's outside our scope. But there's a lot of knowledge needed to care for water, any water, to keep it clear and clean for fish and plants. Unfortunately, that particular family was always small and now they are old, except for the Youth, and minding water is too strenuous for them.'

'What has the Youth done to become a black shadow?' asked Minty.

'Or is it just a matter of what he doesn't do?' asked Coriander.

'He ran away from home,' said Jim. 'Such a thing has never been known before. There's folk who try to reach the Minders' Village and fail. There's none who ever wanted to leave until the Youth ran away to the Hilltop Town. It caused a lot of talk at the time and, would you believe it, there were some people who were glad at our shame? There are those, you see, who don't like the Minders, who consider then priggish and interfering busybodies—' Jim stopped talking again, this time from amazement that this could be so.

Jan gave Coriander a sly nudge. He remembered what she had said about not wanting any Minder looking after her herbs. Coriander pretended not to notice.

'How does the Youth earn his living?' asked Araminta.

'Catch as catch can,' replied Jim, so Minty still didn't know.

'I can't think why he hasn't joined Albert and Sidney before this,' Jim went on, 'he's fond enough of ruffianly company.'

Araminta remembered how Jim and Fred had described Albert and Sidney.

'Does the Youth wear flashy clothes and have inconsiderate manners?' she asked.

'The Youth's clothes are *indescribably* vulgar,' answered Jim, 'his manners are worse and there's also the matter of his hair.'

'What's wrong with that?' asked Coriander.

'Hangs down his back like a great yellow bush,' said Jim. 'And can you believe this? I've seen that Youth sitting, just sitting, combing that hair like, like a mermaid.'

Nobody liked to laugh, Jim looked so upset.

'And now that the Youth has joined Albert and Sidney no one will be safe in the Village. Now, not only are Nathaniel's clocks in danger, but our whole way of life.'

'Surely all the Minders together can protect themselves against three men?' said Jan.

Jim replied that this was true, but until now no one had been able to reach the Village unless a Minder had shown them the way; and never before had there been a renegade Minder, so they were safe. Now there was the Youth. He might take any riff-raff to the Village for a big enough reward. Taking Albert and Sidney could be the start of a reign of terror. Why, he might even take Ripper Tooth and Scarifier. When everyone asked who they were, Jim said that if he gave a true account of those two devil's children no one would have a wink of sleep. And he wouldn't say another word. Instead, he suggested that Wayfarer should join them in their journey to the Minders' Village.

Wayfarer said the Village was a place he had long wanted to visit, even though there was no question of mapping the route.

'No,' agreed Jim, 'there's never been a map drawn of the path across the Blue Hills and perhaps there never will; but I'll draw you a map to add to your collection—a map that no one else possesses or ever could possess. A map that will be unique.'

No one, Araminta thought, could call Jim modest. Or Horace Tompkins.

'A map that's unique,' repeated Wayfarer, and his face glowed with such delight that Minty knew maps meant as much to him as poems did to Jan and herbs to Coriander and inventions to Grandfather Ganderglas.

'And yet the map won't be of the Winding Way over the Blue Hills?' said Wayfarer, remembering that Jim had said this route would never be mapped.

'No,' said Jim, 'My map won't show the path over the hills, but under them.'

'Under the Blue Hills?' whispered Minty. 'You mean people walk under these hills?'

'Not now because the way up to the Empty Plain has been blocked, but when the Youth's family was young and vigorous, his father minded the Silent River that runs underneath. Then there was constant traffic down there. In bad weather, when snow lay in drifts across the Winding Way, Minders walked by the side of the Silent River halfway to the Hilltop Town. The river changes course there and flows out to sea. And at that point there used to be a way up to the Plain. Now this opening is closed, just as the entrance down to the caverns is closed. There has to be someone down there if people use the river path—otherwise, if folk had a fall they might lie there and freeze to death. Had the Youth been willing to take on his father's work, we would still be using the river way.'

'Couldn't someone else carry on the work?' asked Coriander.

'Minders very rarely take over one another's jobs. They're bred to one branch of our occupation over generations.'

'How do you know the path well enough to draw a map?' asked Wayfarer.

'At one time I went down there every day. The Youth's father taught me all the twists and turns of that river—the main stream and the different tributaries that lead only to lakes of ice. For a long time that was the route I used to the Hilltop Town. But like everyone else, I had to stop when the Youth's father retired. I doubt if any of the young generation of Minders has even seen the purple waters of the Indigo Pool.'

'Purple water?' they echoed.

'Not only is the water purple, but anyone who falls in comes out the same colour.'

'Even after a few minutes?' asked Jan.

'Even after a few seconds,' said Jim.

'Purple hair?'

'Yes.'

'Purple nose?'

'Yes.'

'Purple teeth?'

'For *always*?' asked Minty. 'For *ever*?'

'Oh no, not for ever but long enough; the Youth's great-grandfather once cooled his feet in the Indigo Pool and they had a blackberry tinge for at least six months.'

'No wonder people don't go near the Indigo Pool,' observed Coriander, 'though I daresay if I really looked into the matter I could find a herb to restore the skin more quickly.'

'Blow a purple nose,' sang Jan.

'Shake a purple hand, ' sang Coriander.

'Wipe a purple tear,' sang Minty.

'Brush a purple beard,' growled Wayfarer in his deep voice.

And so, while Jim drew Wayfarer a map of the Silent River and its course through the icy caverns, the others sang their song of the Indigo Pool and drank rice and raisin wine and quite forgot their spirits had ever dropped to their boots.

6

Early the next morning they set off along the Winding Way. Jim had finished his map showing the secret course of the Silent River through the icy caverns, and Wayfarer had put this away in his pack. Wayfarer held that map as other people might hold a fistful of precious stones. Then he put his pack in the carriage beside the provisions and the family's change of clothes.

Jim, whose leg was quite well again, walked beside Misery, and the others followed behind the carriage, one after the other.

At first Minty thought the path felt ordinary, just like any other, and then she changed her mind. There was a feeling about those hills and that path that wasn't ordinary at all.

As they walked, sometimes talking, sometimes singing, sometimes in silence, Araminta felt she was a long way from anywhere that was familiar—a long way from the great church on the Empty Plain and Fred Steeple; a long way from the Hilltop Town, from the Ox Drove and from the Old House, where Grandfather Ganderglas and Aunt Tilly Humble would be busy doing practical jobs.

Coriander found two new wild flowers as they walked along. She was pleased by this discovery, but annoyed that there should be gaps in her knowledge. Coriander was like that.

The hills were all round them now. Some were high and some were low. Some were green with grass and some grey with flint and boulder and some really were blue. The Winding Way curled like a pig's tail round them all.

As they walked, Minty noticed that Jim kept glancing at the sky. So Minty looked up there, too, and saw some very threatening grey clouds nudging the fat and cheerful white ones. Worse, clouds of wispy black hung like rags in front of the grey. The sun had squeezed into one narrow crack between all these clouds, shining down on a single hill. Wayfarer pointed to the brilliance of this hill.

'Beautiful,' said Jan, and everyone sighed for his impractical nature. Everyone but Jan knew there was a storm coming.

'Why don't we put up the tents for shelter?' suggested Minty, and Coriander said how lucky that Araminta had inherited a practical streak from her Grandfather Ganderglas and Aunt Tilly Humble. Minty thought she would like to be able to write poems like Jan.

'We'll leave the carriage here,' said Jim, 'covered by one of the tents and then climb to higher ground.'

Jim loosed Misery from the carriage while Jan took out the four tents.

They fastened one over the carriage and carried the others further up the hill. Now the sun had gone, leaving the hill that had been so brilliant as dark as the others. Soon, a few drops of rain sprinkled their heads.

'Hurry,' said Coriander, but the hill was steep and soon the rain was falling faster, blowing into their eyes. When they reached a bend in the hills Jim said they had better stop and put up the tents. This was easy to say and hard to do. As fast as Jan and Jim and Wayfarer put up the tents, the wind blew them down. And all the while the rain drove into their faces. At last the tents were up. O Misery Me and Wag sheltered in one, Wayfarer and Jim in another and the Humbles in the third.

Moments later the wind whirled into a frenzy, thunder rumbled from hill to hill and as for the lightning! Minty had never seen anything so bright as the lightning that flew from under the clouds, not even on November the 5th. The tents rattled and shook and every now and then, when the gusts of wind were particularly fierce, the canvas blew out like a sail.

'I'm not *frightened*,' said Minty, who was, 'but what if these tents blow down?'

'We'll put them up again,' said Jan, and struggled outside to make sure that Misery and Wag were all right. Jim and Wayfarer were having a look, too. Misery and Wag were huddled together inside their tent, Misery's nose resting on Wag's head.

Jan and Wayfarer and Jim were soaked just by going from one tent to the other.

Afterwards, they learned that such a storm had never been known before. In the Hilltop Town that storm was talked about for weeks—everyone had a different tale of how washing had been torn from the line before there was time to take it in; how tiles had come tumbling off roof-tops and chimneys had crashed to the ground. Afterwards, that storm became a legend, the subject of songs and stories: but no one thought of songs and stories while the thunder crashed about and the rain pelted down.

The storm had started at noon and stopped at three in the afternoon. Then the sun crept out, steaming the sides of the tents and turning the Blue Hills into sapphires. The brilliance of those hills made everybody's eyes ache.

They decided to let the tents dry off a bit before taking

them down, and Coriander suggested a bite of pie while they waited.

They walked carefully down the wet hillside, but the joy they felt because the storm was over soon turned to deepest dismay. Jim made the discovery first. As he drew near the carriage he gave an exclamation. Then ran forward.

'We've been robbed!' cried Jim.

They all rushed forward. The tent that had covered the carriage was no longer there. They crowded round, staring inside. Only Misery's oats were there. Otherwise, the carriage was empty. Stores gone. Spare clothing gone. Wayfarer's pack gone. Nothing remained but the pink velvet cushion, sodden with rain.

'Perhaps the wind blew the tent away,' said Jan.

'Impossible,' said Jim. 'Besides, if the storm was to blame, some of our things would still be here; or lying about somewhere. No, Albert and Sidney and the Youth have passed this way. They've stolen everything.'

'All my maps,' whispered Wayfarer, 'all my maps.'

No one said a word. They knew that no words could comfort Wayfarer in such a disaster. Wayfarer's maps were his love and his life. It was as though Coriander had found her herb garden empty, or Grandfather Ganderglas all his inventions stolen. Minty thought Jan the luckiest. Poetry can't be stolen, only poems; and Jan didn't care about his once they were written down.

'They haven't even left the syrup of borage,' said Coriander, who would have liked to give Wayfarer a stiff dose of it.

'I wonder,' said Jan, 'whether they were on their way to or from the Village? If they were on their way back to the Hilltop Town that might mean they have also stolen Nathaniel's clocks.'

'We must catch them without delay,' Jim said, 'to retrieve Wayfarer's maps and find out about the clocks.'

'I'll go back to the Hilltop Town,' said Wayfarer, 'while the rest of you go on to the Minders' Village. That way, one of us is bound to find them or hear news of them.'

No one would allow this. They all began talking at once, saying that Wayfarer would be taking far too great a risk, going alone in pursuit of those three. Wayfarer replied that he was used to taking risks. He had encountered more than one villain on his travels. If Albert and Sidney and the Youth succeeded in reaching the Hilltop Town, there would be little hope of retrieving clocks or maps. Everyone knew this was true, but no one wanted Wayfarer to travel alone. On the other hand, if the family accompanied Wayfarer this would leave Jim by himself. What a fix.

Wayfarer had a very determined character, however, and was on the point of turning back, regardless of what anyone said, when Jim gave an exclamation.

'Now what?' asked Jan. Jim's exclamations always seemed a sign of trouble.

'I've just thought,' replied Jim, 'supposing those villains open Wayfarer's pack? Suppose they look at his maps and find the one I've drawn of the Silent River? That map could give the Youth the idea of reaching the Hilltop Town by the underground route, especially if they have stolen Nathaniel's clocks. When the robbery is discovered the Winding Way will be crowded with Minders searching for the three of them; but there's no danger of pursuit in the caverns beside the river.'

'But you said there was no longer a way up from the underground river to the Empty Plain,' said Coriander.

'The Youth may think that Wayfarer has cleared one. He will see from the maps that Wayfarer's business is clearing paths and opening up closed entrances. The Youth isn't a fool.' Jim said this reluctantly.

'Then they will have to walk back to the entrance again,' said Jan, 'and come along the Winding Way after all.'

'If they can find their way back to the entrance,' replied Jim, his tone ominous. 'They won't find their way forward very easily, even with the map; they could be lost in the caverns for ever more coming backwards.'

Coriander spoke in her most practical Ganderglas voice.

'Clearly,' she said, 'we must go down there ourselves to look for them. We can't risk leaving them to perish.'

Everyone agreed with this, although Jim was heard to mutter that they wouldn't be much loss, but then they started arguing about who should go. Jim thought he should go alone; the others wouldn't hear of this. Jan thought he and Jim and Wayfarer should go. Coriander wouldn't hear of this. So finally they all decided to go and then Wag started barking in case they'd forgotten him; which they had. And when they decided to take Wag, there was the problem of Misery. There seemed to be nothing but problems. Finally they decided to leave Misery at the entrance to the underground river and hope to find her there when they came up again. Misery, who understood well enough, looked disgusted, but Minty told her she was fortunate that the thieves had at least left her food alone.

To reach the entrance down to the river they had to walk deep into the hills. First, however, they returned to the tents, took them down, rolled them and put them in the carriage, hiding them under the seat. Then they set off, trying to forget they hadn't had any lunch and might not have any supper.

When they were so far into the Blue Hills that it was

hard to tell where the hills finished and the sky began, so alike were they in colour, Jim began looking for the entrance to the river.

'Ah!' he said, 'we were right.' He pointed to a great blue rock. 'Someone has rolled that rock away—it's blocked the entrance since the Youth's father retired. That's the entrance.' He pointed to a dark hole in the ground.

They all stared at this black opening with some dismay and wondered whether searching for Albert and Sidney and the Youth was such a good idea after all. Perhaps they didn't need rescuing. Perhaps they weren't even down there.

Jim knelt in front of the hole.

'Look—their footprints—and there are more on the steps.'

When the others peered down the hole, they saw a flight of old, worn, mossy steps. Down, down, down, went those steps into the darkness. And down the steps went Jim, calling all sorts of warnings and do be carefuls over his shoulder as the others followed one by one.

At first those steps seemed very dark, especially after the brilliance of the sun shining on the Blue Hills. Presently a strange, eerie, sunless light crept up towards them, the kind of thin glimmering that rises from water; and there was the river flowing swift and silent below them. That river was quieter than a mouse holding its breath.

A few moments later they stood in the icy caverns that rose around the Silent River. Those caverns would chill the stoutest, warmest heart. They glittered ice blue and white, shining with the pale, luminous light of water and they were still. As still as they were silent. O it was a strange place. Not a place for people at all. Not even for fishes. Minty didn't see so much as the flick of a fin in those freezing waters.

Jim said they must leave a trail behind them as they walked. Otherwise, even he couldn't be sure of finding the way back. Of course no one had anything to leave a trail with, so Jan suggested leaving crosses on the floor of the cavern. Jan was never without a pencil.

Every step they took carried them further and further, deeper and deeper underground. The river no longer flowed straight. There were twists and turns and presently they came to a meeting place of caverns and tributaries—a place where you could walk in a dozen directions and not know whether you were following the river or one of the tributaries.

'Let's hope,' said Jim, 'that those rogues took the right path.'

Now the river was half covered by ledges of rock. The

path was narrow, too. And the ceiling of rock was lower. Sometimes they had to bend their heads. Sometimes they had to crawl over pools and streams. And all the time they were cold and hungry and frightened of getting lost.

'Listen!' said Minty suddenly.

No one else could hear a thing.

'I can hear the ticking of a clock,' said Minty.

This news amazed everyone. They stood still, listening, and soon they, too, heard ticking—scarcely louder than a grasshopper rubbing his legs together.

'And there's the clock,' cried Minty. She bent down and picked up what the others would have taken for a stone. Instead, it was a tiny marble clock—the smallest clock anyone had ever seen.

'So they have robbed Nathaniel,' said Jim. 'That's his clock without doubt. They must have dropped it.'

As he spoke the clock chimed. Minty had never heard such a gentle, merry, musical sound. She handed Jim the clock, but he told her that he knew Nathaniel would say the clock was hers. So she put it into her pocket, where she could just hear it ticking; like an extra heart.

'Look!' said Jan.

'Not another clock?' they all asked.

'No,' replied Jan, 'look at the water—the colour's changing.'

He was quite right. The water was no longer an icy grey but blue, deep blue, almost violet.

'We must be near the Indigo Pool,' said Jim.

Hardly had he spoken than they heard a tremendous commotion. Harsh, quarrelling voices, all shouting together.

'They're by the Indigo Pool,' said Jim. No need to ask who. Albert, Sidney and the Youth, without doubt. The travellers paused. They had to; the path was blocked by a rock so large that to continue their journey they would have to climb over the top, a difficult, slippery business, or creep round the edge. No one knew which would be the more difficult. But the rock was useful as well as awkward: without that rock Albert and Sidney and the Youth would have seen the travellers instantly. They decided to look over the top and see what lay on the other side. No one could have called them skilled mountaineers. They made the most terrible to-do about climbing that rock, with Jim constantly putting his finger to his lips for less noise and more stealth, and Coriander losing her balance and clutching at Jan and Minty, and Wag tripping everyone up just when they reached the top. At last they were safely there and peering over the top. There lay the Indigo Pool, a still and circular lake of deepest, richest purple. On the edge of the lake, on the smooth, hard rock of the path, lay a sack. Bulging. No need to ask what was inside. The chiming and cuckooing and tick-tocking that came from that sack was almost as loud as the voices of Albert and Sidney and the Youth.

Albert, Sidney and the Youth, standing beside the sack, didn't notice the five faces—six, counting Wag—watching them over the top of the rock. They were too busy shouting at one another. Besides, they were certain they were alone in those icy caverns.

The Youth was unmistakable. He was the youngest, the biggest and the noisiest. His bush of yellow hair hung down his back just as Jim had said. He wore striped trousers, and a shirt decorated with palm trees and embroidered with the words 'Hurrah for Wasp and Gloucester.' Wasp and Gloucester, Jim said, lived in the Hilltop Town, and had given the Youth free lodging. Goodness knows why, said Jim.

Minty supposed Jim was right in thinking the Youth's

clothes indescribably vulgar: but they were cheerful, too.

The Youth was holding Jim's map and Wayfarer's pack hung from his shoulder. Jim had to restrain Wayfarer from dashing forward there and then.

'Wait,' counselled Jim.

Albert and Sidney were older than the Youth, and not so wild; more mean and calculating.

'The one in the velvet suit is Albert,' whispered Jim.

Albert was holding Grandfather's tent, very carelessly rolled, as though he were about to hit someone. The more the Youth shouted, the tighter became Albert's grip on that tent.

'I tell you,' roared the Youth, 'that the hills will be full of Minders looking for us; and the Plain, too, most probably. We'll go as far as the entrance to the Empty Plain, but we won't go up to the Plain until dark.'

'And I tell you,' shouted Albert, 'that if we stay down here until nightfall we'll freeze to death. I'm freezing now.' And indeed he had begun dancing up and down, though whether from cold or rage it was hard to say.

'Stay down here if you like,' snarled Sidney to the Youth. 'We're going on to the Hilltop Town without any more delays; so show us the way to the entrance.'

'If I stay down here, my good friends,' said the Youth, suddenly quiet and lofty (and talking nonsense because Albert and Sidney had never been good friends to anyone), 'and stay here until nightfall is what I intend to do, these clocks stay with me.'

'Those clocks are ours,' roared Sidney, 'we stole them. You can have the two we said you could have.'

'Two!' sneered the Youth. 'Two out of forty! You wouldn't have reached the Village without me. Two! Three into forty goes—' He stopped, clearly having no idea how many times three went into forty, then said: 'must be eleven or twelve times, so that's twelve clocks each.'

Albert made a snatch at the map which the Youth still held in his hand. The Youth whisked it away. Then he put one foot on the sack of clocks and one hand on his hip.

'If you want the map,' said the Youth, 'come and get it. Likewise, if you want the clocks, come and get them.'

'All right,' shouted Albert and Sidney, 'we will.' And they rushed at the Youth, Albert brandishing the rolled-up tent and Sidney whirling his arms.

The Youth didn't care. He knew he was bigger and stronger and a better fighter than either of those two. A moment later the thud of blows and the echo of harsh voices resounded throughout those otherwise silent caverns. Soon all that could be seen was the thrashing of arms and legs

and all that could be heard was grunts and groans and bad words. Then they were in a heap on top of the sack. No one quite saw what happened next, but there was a mighty splash and the three of them and the sack as well vanished under the purple surface of the Indigo Pool.

'Fools!' cried Jim. 'The clocks will be ruined and so will all Wayfarer's maps.' Because, of course, the pack had gone in with the Youth.

Jim climbed over the rock and the others followed. Wag splashed round the edge, through the water, and his paws were tinged blue for months.

As they stood at the edge of the Indigo Pool, staring in, three heads shot up out of the water. Purple heads.

Albert, Sidney and the Youth climbed out, purple.

'Look at you,' cried Albert to Sidney, 'what a sight! Are you ill? You're purple as a plum.'

'What about you?' cried Sidney in reply. 'Purple to your corns I shouldn't wonder.'

They both looked at the Youth.

'Him, too,' said Albert. 'What's happened to us? Have we caught nettlerash?'

'You've been dyed by the purple waters of the Indigo Pool,' said Jim.

'Purple!' shouted Sidney, 'how can we be purple burglars? We're marked men. Our whole livelihood is ruined.'

'Then you'd better find another,' Jim said. 'And about time, too.'

'My hair,' wailed the Youth, 'what about my hair?'

'Purple as a blackberry bush,' said Jim. 'Didn't you remember about the Indigo Pool? Don't you remember anything you've been taught?'

The Youth was holding handfuls of hair in front of his eyes so that he could see exactly what colour it was.

'What do you intend to do about the clocks?' demanded Jim. 'The sack is still at the bottom of the lake—with Wayfarer's pack and the Humbles' tent.'

'And there they can stay for all I care,' said the Youth.

Wayfarer was taking off his cloak.

'A purple skin won't make much difference to me,' he said. 'I'll get the clocks.' And without further ado, before anyone could stop him, he plunged into the Indigo Pool. Up he came again, purple as the others, and threw his pack and the tent on to the rocky bank.

'I'll have to go back for the clocks,' he said, 'the sack was too heavy to bring up with one hand.'

'I'll go this time,' cried Jim, 'you'll get double dyed.'

But Wayfarer had dived back under the water, leaving only a trail of wine-coloured bubbles.

Jim was right. When Wayfarer struggled to the surface with the sack, his face was double dyed. Everyone was silent at the sight of him.

Jim held out his hand and grasped Wayfarer's, helping him out of the water. Jan dragged the sack to the bank; so both Jim and Jan had violet hands, but that was nothing to the colour of Wayfarer.

Jim opened the sack and took out the clocks. Each one was purple. Afterwards, those clocks became the most famous and the most greatly admired of all Nathaniel's clocks, but at that moment everyone stared at them in greatest dismay. They were still ticking and chiming, however, and even while they watched, the door of a cuckoo clock sprang open and out flew a purple cuckoo.

The Youth had sunk down on to the rock in a state of

deepest melancholia. Looking at his terrible gloom, Coriander remembered the borage.

'What happened to our stores?' she asked.

'Ate the pie,' said the Youth.

'And the herbs?'

'Herbs?' said the Youth vaguely.

In fact, the herbs had been dropped among the hills, where they took root and flourish to this day. The syrup of borage, of course, had simply sunk into the ground.

'Perhaps if you cut off your hair,' Minty said to the Youth, 'the new hair will grow yellow.'

The Youth looked a shade more cheerful.

'I know,' he said, 'I'll dye my skin with a walnut dye and everyone will think I've been to the South Seas.'

'Better still,' said Jim 'go to the South Seas.'

'We could sue you for this,' Sidney told the youth. 'We're finished as professional men until this colour wears off.'

'What about me?' said the Youth.

'You're a professional man,' said Albert. 'A professional layabout, that's all you are.'

'I only hope,' said Jim to the Youth, 'that these experiences will discourage you from taking *riff-raff* to the Village'—he said 'riff-raff' with a terrible contemptuous look at Albert and Sidney.

'Oh, stop nagging,' said the Youth crossly. 'Isn't my downfall enough for you?'

'I like to get things quite clear,' said Jim.

Coriander said it was time they turned back; that Wayfarer would catch pneumonia in his wet clothes. This gave the Youth another fright. Albert and Sidney didn't look too happy either. Very quietly, they turned and walked on, as though hoping they wouldn't be noticed.

'No need to think you can sneak back to the Hilltop

Town by the entrance from these caverns to the Plain, even if you could find the way. The entrance is still closed. That's why we came down here— to find you all before you were irretrievably lost.'

'Closed!' shouted Albert and Sidney together. *'Closed!'*

'Hasn't he opened it?' demanded the Youth, pointing at Wayfarer in his rude way. 'That's his job, isn't it? Opening up paths?'

'That's his job,' agreed Jim, 'but he hasn't opened the way to the Plain because he didn't know such an opening existed. He didn't know about the river. I drew that map.'

If those three hadn't been so wet and cold and dispirited there would have been another fight.

'You'd better come back to the Village,' Jim said to the Youth, 'if you want to go into hiding until your hair grows yellow again. No doubt all will be forgiven. Though if you were my son it wouldn't.' He looked round at Albert and Sidney. 'If we had such a thing as a jail, which I am glad to say we haven't, you'd be inside all right.'

Albert and Sidney glared at him.

Minty was glad the Youth would be coming to the Village. There was something about him she liked. It would be hard to say what exactly. But something.

They were all longing to be finished with those icy, echoing caverns, but the way back to the steps seemed very long; perhaps because everyone felt so hungry.

Wayfarer was looking very pinched. A trail of purple drips followed him, staining the smooth rock of their path. They felt a little in awe of Wayfarer now. So much courage and so little vanity. But Wayfarer asked why they were staring at him like that: if his friends stared, he said, what would strangers do?

'Misery will be glad to see us,' Minty said when at last

they reached the steps. But when they had climbed them and stood again among the hills, breathing deeply of the cool, sweet air which still smelled of rain but was now warmed by sun, Misery was nowhere to be seen. Until Minty caught a glimpse of her dismal tail whisking at a fly.

Misery was walking away with a fat little man dressed in checked riding breeches and a diamond patterned shirt, like a jockey's.

'Look, look,' cried Minty, 'a man's taking Misery away. He's not Ripper Tooth or Scarifier, is he Jim?'

Jim laughed. 'No, that's Alfie Wildlife, who looks after abandoned animals.' He put his hands to his mouth and shouted Alfie's name.

Alfie turned, then came walking towards them. Misery walked with him. The Humbles felt very hurt that she should go off like that with a perfect stranger.

Alfie Wildlife was the fattest Minder Minty had seen so

far. She didn't think he could do as much walking as the others. She learned later that he didn't do any. There was always a horse or a donkey to carry him. When Jim had introduced him, he told the Humbles how sorry he was to have thought Misery abandoned. He had been misled, he said, by her sad look. The look of an abandoned animal. The family felt as annoyed as the gypsies had done when they had learned the Humbles thought Misery ill-treated.

Then Jim told Alfie how Wayfarer had rescued the clocks, and Alfie told the travellers how all the Minders were out searching the hills and what a turmoil the burglary had left the village in. Nobody had believed that Albert and Sidney would ever succeed in stealing the clocks. Here Alfie gave the Youth a nasty look, but the Youth didn't notice; yet again he had grasped a handful of his hair and was holding it in front of his eyes. Hoping perhaps that it wasn't quite so purple as he had feared. In the sunshine it was even more purple. The Youth groaned.

'I think your hair looks nice,' said Minty. 'Like a sunset.'

The Youth replied gloomily that he didn't want to look like a sunset.

Alfie walked back with them to the Winding Way. He and Jim had a very earnest discussion which they didn't share with anyone else. Then Alfie left them, after an admiring speech to Wayfarer. Minty could see that Wayfarer became very embarrassed with speeches of this kind.

The news that the clocks had been rescued reached the Village more quickly than the travellers. Word sped along the Winding Way and among the hills, where the Minders were still searching. Every now and then one or two would come to Jim to be introduced to the family and to shake Wayfarer by the hand.

Minty noticed that whenever this happened, Jim took the

Minder to one side for a lot of whispering and quiet talk behind the hand. The Humbles pretended not to notice. Presently Jim turned to them. He had the look of a man with something important to say.

'The time is now six o'clock,' he said, and everyone felt this a very poor opening remark. He went on: 'We shall reach the village in about fifteen minutes. If you then rested, would you be ready for a celebration banquet at midnight?'

They assured him they would feel absolutely like that; Coriander murmured that she wouldn't mind a small banquet before resting, but Jan coughed loudly so that no one should hear.

Just before they reached the Village they saw Alfie Wildlife again. He galloped past on the biggest, strongest horse the travellers had ever seen—a great grey horse with mane that blew silver in the wind.

'That's Grailing,' Jim told them. A smaller horse ran beside them and she was brown as autumn bracken. Alfie had rescued them both from being sold for horse meat. Everyone shuddered, and Coriander said surely a magnificent horse like Grailing would never have been in danger of the knacker's yard. Jim said that Grailing had looked very different before living for a year with Alfie.

'Has he any more abandoned horses?' asked Minty.

'I expect so. Alfie always has a horse or two. Alfie has every kind of animal: cats that were bundled out of houses as kittens, dogs that no one wants. You'd never believe the number of abandoned animals there are. And then there are pheasants that have been wounded by the gun but fell where no hunter or dog could find them; foxes that escaped the hounds but were injured in the chase; and hounds turned out of the pack because they're too old to hunt.'

Alfie had other animals—animals that had been loved

and cherished by families but stolen by villains. Jim gave another nasty look at the Youth when he said this; Jim couldn't leave that Youth alone. Minty felt sure the Youth would never steal an animal.

'Why do you want to know whether Alfie has another horse, Minty?' asked Coriander.

'I thought he might be able to give us one for our stables,' Minty replied.

'We couldn't have just one,' said Jan. 'He'd be lonely.'

'Two then,' said Minty.

'But what when we have to move on from the Old House?' said Jan. 'What if the next house we're caretakers in has no stable? Where should we put two horses and a donkey?'

Wag barked. So he meant to stay, too.

'Leave the Old House,' whispered Araminta, 'we can't do that—ever.'

'We shall have to,' said Jan. 'The Old House isn't ours, never could be; we haven't enough money to buy the gate-posts. The Old House belongs to Mr Richard Arthur Edmund Cressington.'

'Perhaps you'll find another house you like as well,' said Wayfarer. 'Either to look after or have for yourselves.'

'Never,' shouted the Humbles, 'never, never never.'

When they first saw the Minders' Village, they were all a little disappointed. As Jim had told Araminta, it looked like any other village and not so pretty as some; the cottages were like cottages anywhere. Yet, after a while, like the Winding Way, that village didn't feel ordinary at all. Later, Minty decided that the feel of the Village was like the feel of one of Jan's poems; the truth was there, and real

life was there, but not the sort of real life you meet with every day.

Nathaniel, with Fergusson his cat, was waiting to greet them, just at the point where the Winding Way reached the first cottage.

Nathaniel was just as Jim had described him; a very little, very old, very gentle man, dressed in a thin yellow woollen suit covered by a dark green cloak. His polka dot hat he carried under his arm.

Nathaniel had been standing there for some time, practising his thank you speech. But when Jim introduced him to the Humbles and to Wayfarer, all he could do was to shake each of them by the hand. He knew what he wanted to say, especially to Wayfarer, but he could hardly manage a word. Unlike most of the other Minders, Nathaniel simply wasn't a talker. He and Fergusson lived very quiet lives.

Fergusson stayed aloof while Nathaniel struggled with his gratitude. Fergusson still felt badly about his failure to protect the clocks. He had been out hunting at the time. Fergusson had orange fur striped black, flashing amber eyes and whiskers that curled in a dozen directions. Fergusson had a look of ferocity.

Finally, Nathaniel gave up trying to make a speech: Wayfarer told him he considered himself privileged to rescue the clocks and what did having a purple skin for a while matter?

Araminta showed Nathaniel the clock she had found, and Nathaniel said of course she must keep it. Then Jim told the Humbles that although Wayfarer would stay with him, they were to rest in Alfie Wildlife's cottage. Alfie's cottage was the biggest in the Village. Besides, Alfie wouldn't be home until midnight. Jim refused absolutely to say where he'd gone.

When Alfie did return, he made a tremendous din which was just as well; the Humbles might not have woken up for the banquet otherwise. They would simply have gone on sleeping. No one could have slept through Alfie's return. There were loud cries of 'Whoa, there' amid the clatter and stamp of Grailing's feet, and the whinnying of the little brown mare.

There was the stamp of human feet, too, several pairs of them, but the Humbles took no interest in these. The Humbles were too busy stretching and yawning and washing and talking.

Coriander was wishing she had a proper celebration dress to wear.

Araminta was wishing she didn't feel so sleepy and wondering what happened at celebrations. She asked Jan. Jan said eating and drinking happened; sometimes singing and dancing, too. And speeches. Jan said he only hoped he wouldn't have to make one.

Coriander, Jan and Minty all said what a pity that Grandfather Ganderglas and Aunt Tilly Humble couldn't be there. They were convivial by nature, those two, and there's very little opportunity for social blossoming when you follow the caretaking profession.

The Humbles went down the stairs as Alfie came in.

'Hullo there,' he called.

Coriander wondered whether they would have to wait while Alfie changed his riding breeches and jockey's shirt and how long he would take to do this. Coriander was punctual by nature. Alfie, however, clearly didn't intend to bother with any changing.

'Just wash my hands,' he said, 'and we'll get along. Hope you're rested?'

They assured him they were quite rested and Coriander said, for politeness' sake, what a nice house he had.

'Isn't it pleasant?' agreed Alfie carelessly. 'Not cluttered, that's what I like.'

Alfie's house certainly wasn't cluttered. Bare as a bone, really. Just a few tables and chairs, many pictures, all crookedly hung, and half empty pots of Gentleman's Relish wherever you cared to look. Not a speck of polish anywhere, and as for extras like chairbacks and curtains—Alfie wouldn't have known what you were talking about. The night sky came sweeping right into Alfie's house. Minty half expected to see stars lying about the floor.

'Where are all your abandoned animals?' she asked Alfie.

They had only seen one dog, asleep in the kitchen.

Alfie said the animals mostly slept in the stables. They

liked to be all together. Wag and O Misery Me were out there, too, getting acquainted.

Araminta said she would like to meet Grailing and Alfie promised to introduce her the next day: to Grailing and to all the other animals. That would take most of the day, Alfie said.

The celebration was to be held in the Mayor's Parlour. In the Minders' Village there was a mayor's parlour but no mayor. No one had time for ceremonial. But everyone thought a dignified name was needed for the building used for their merriest, their most important and their most solemn happenings.

The street was empty as they walked from Alfie's house to the Mayor's Parlour. Minty had never set out for anywhere in the middle of the night before. It gave her a back to front feeling, but enjoyable.

'Expect we'll be the last to arrive,' said Alfie, who always was. 'Look, there's the Mayor's Parlour . . .'

No need to point it out. The Mayor's Parlour looked and sounded as though a dozen celebrations were going on. The brilliant lights, the bunting, the crowd and the clamour made the Humbles shy of going in.

Alfie, on the other hand, looked keen.

'I do like a banquet,' he confided. 'Now come and meet everyone. Although—' here he paused—*'although there are some present you already know.'*

The Humbles couldn't think why he spoke so emphatically and mysteriously. They thought he was referring to Jim and Wayfarer—who were waiting just inside the open door.

Wayfarer wasn't allowed simply to stand and wait. Everyone who passed shook his purple hand. Minders are great handshakers. Once wasn't enough. They all shook Wayfarer's hand each time they passed.

Alfie, however, hadn't meant Jim and Wayfarer when he told the Humbles they would know some of those present. There, beaming away behind Jim and Wayfarer, were Grandfather Ganderglas, Aunt Tilly Humble, Horace Tompkins and Fred Steeple.

'How . . . ?' 'What . . . ?' 'Where . . . ?' 'Who . . . ?' stuttered the Humbles.

Alfie Wildlife looked complacent.

'Grailing and I fetched them,' he said, 'and the little brown mare.'

'So that's where you went.' cried the Humbles. 'But how did you manage to get there and back in time?'

'Grailing moves like the shadow of a cloud crossing a hillside,' said Alfie. Grailing always brought out Alfie's poetic streak. 'And the little mare is as fast, although she hasn't the staying power, of course. I left her at the great church for Fred.'

'You mean Grailing carried Father and Tilly and you and Horace?' asked Coriander.

'That's nothing to Grailing,' scoffed Alfie.

'What a rush we had,' said Grandfather Ganderglas. 'No time to put on our best.'

'No need either,' said Alfie.

'Now don't you start worrying about the house,' said Tilly to the family. 'Mr Wildlife—'

'Alfie, if you please,' he interrupted.

'Alfie brought Mr Lampington with him to stay until our return.'

'The one Minder who doesn't enjoy a good celebration,' said Alfie. 'His people have always looked after lighthouses, you know, and I suppose the loneliness has given them a solitary outlook on life.'

'I've been given one of Nathaniel's clocks,' Minty told Aunt Tilly Humble, 'so we needn't listen out for Mr Figge's cattle any more.'

'Figge is so angry with me,' said Grandfather, laughing, 'that if he knew we listened out for his cattle he'd probably cover their hooves with woollen socks to muffle the sound.' And he told them about his battle, and his victory, over the deer traps.

Minty's clock wasn't the only one that Nathaniel gave to the Humbles. He gave them a mighty grandfather clock (which presented a terrible transport problem) painted with scenes from the Winding Way and the Empty Plain, with glimpses of the great church and the Hilltop Town and even the Ox Drove. This clock not only struck the hours and half hours and quarter hours but, since Nathaniel had hidden a musical box inside, played many a tinkling tune as well.

But that clock wasn't given to the Humbles until later, after this story finishes. So far, the celebration hadn't started. The Minders had still to be introduced to the Humbles. This became very confusing because they all insisted on being introduced several times, with non-stop handshaking.

The banquet started without anyone really noticing. No one sits down at a Minders' banquet. A Minder likes to eat walking about as a Scotsman likes to eat his porridge off a mantelshelf.

Even Aunt Tilly Humble was aghast at the size of the banquet. All the Minders had emptied their larders for the occasion. There were delicacies of every kind; and several pots of Gentleman's Relish from Alfie. Flagons of wine, too, all home-brewed.

A Minder's idea of a banquet isn't just eating and drinking.

Their idea of a banquet includes talking and laughing, singing and dancing, and making speeches. At Minders' banquets everyone makes a speech; not one after the other, but all together, so that everyone talks and no one has to listen.

Jim waited while a lot of this went on, while goodies vanished from the table and the wine was drunk, while Minty asked Fred Steeple about the great church and the Humbles told Grandfather Ganderglas and Aunt Tilly Humble about their journey, and Grandfather and Tilly told the Humbles about Wayfarer's visit and Horace Tompkins said how exceptionally pleasant he found life at the Old House. Jim Larchington became quite anxious on hearing this. It was bad enough that Fred Steeple had decided never to leave the great church—the Minders couldn't risk Horace Tompkins settling down as well. So Jim, who had something to say of exceptional interest, decided to say it. He clapped his hands, stamped his feet and banged the nearly empty table.

'Friends,' he shouted, 'an announcement!'

This would keep them quiet for a moment or two. Minders are very curious by nature. Each Minder considers it a point of honour to be first with whatever news is going.

'An announcement that gives me much pleasure,' went on Jim.

'Come to the point,' shouted all the Minders.

Jim looked disappointed. He had hoped to turn his announcement into a speech, but the others weren't having any of that. If Jim Larchington was simply pretending to have an announcement to give himself an excuse for making speeches, they would all make speeches, too.

'All right, all right,' said Jim, 'if you insist on a *naked*

announcement, here it is: we are all agreed that Wayfarer has done everyone, not just Nathaniel, but all of us, a great turn—' Cheers and clapping and stamping—'SO' bellowed Jim above the din, 'we have a suggestion to make to him and would you all keep QUIET or he won't hear what the suggestion is.'

Instant quiet. Well, reasonably instant and relatively quiet.

'Wayfarer, the Minders would be honoured if you would accept a cottage in the Village and become a Minder of Tracks and Rights of Way.'

Deafening applause. Then there was real quiet while everyone looked at Wayfarer.

'The greatest honour I could wish for,' said Wayfarer, 'and one I am privileged to accept.'

This time there was a frenzy of clapping and cheering.

The Minders were delighted not only that Wayfarer had agreed to become one of their number, a unique occasion, but that he was so obviously a man of few words. Except for Nathaniel, the Minders liked to talk but not to listen. The Humbles and Grandfather Ganderglas clapped and shouted as loudly as anyone.

They were overjoyed that Wayfarer would now be able to pursue the work he loved but live a less lonely life. No one had liked the thought of Wayfarer sleeping under hedges. Especially in winter.

Wayfarer hadn't quite finished talking after all.

'May I make an announcement?' he asked. (He had quickly grasped the difference between a speech and an announcement.)

Of course, he was told to make as many as he liked.

'This is a happy night for me,' said Wayfarer, 'and I would like to mark it by making a present to my friends Grandfather Ganderglas, Jan and Coriander Humble, Aunt Tilly Humble and Araminta Humble.' (Wayfarer was very careful over matters of precedence). 'Without the Humbles I should probably not have met the Minders. So from gratitude and affection and as a memento of our journey, I would like to give them the Old House.'

A hush. Here was an announcement indeed. Everyone knew the Old House, had seen the countless chimneys on the roof and watched the evening sun turn the windows to a hundred squares of gold. As for the Humbles and Grandfather Ganderglas, no five faces had ever registered such shock before. Open mouths weren't in it.

'You mean . . .' started Jan.

'That you *own* the Old House . . .' said Coriander.

'That you're Richard Arthur Edmund Cressington,' shouted Minty.

'I do happen to have those names,' said Wayfarer, 'Though it's a long time since I used them.'

Wayfarer. To think that Wayfarer—solitary, shabby Wayfarer with his pack of maps, Wayfarer who slept under hedges and hadn't bothered about jumping into the Indigo Pool, was Richard Arthur Edmund Cressington.

And he'd given them the Old House. The house they loved best of any they had ever seen or ever would see. The house with enough room for Grandfather to develop his inventions: the house with kitchens to satisfy even Aunt Tilly Humble: the house where Jan could write his poems and Coriander grow her herbs: the house with a room in the eaves for Minty, where she could tuck herself in like a swallow.

Fred Steeple knew exactly how they were feeling.

'Very nice here,' he whispered to Minty, 'but tomorrow we'll all be on our way home.'

STAY ON

Here are details of other exciting TARGET titles. If you cannot obtain these books from your local bookshop, or newsagent, write to the address below listing the titles you would like and enclosing cheque or postal order—*not* currency—including 7p per book to cover packing and postage; 2–4 books, 5p per copy; 5–8 books, 4p per copy.

TARGET BOOKS,
Universal-Tandem Publishing Co.,
14 Gloucester Road,
London SW7 4RD

ABANDONED! 25p

G. D. Griffiths

0 426 10460 9

A kitten, heartlessly abandoned when 12 weeks old, gradually accepts the loss of her comfort and security, and learns to survive in the grim and savage wilds of storm-racked Dartmoor, several times cheating a cruel death before eventually finding the love and security she secretly longs for. *Illustrated.*

RUNNER-UP TITLE FOR THE 1973 WHITBREAD LITERARY AWARD (CHILDREN'S BOOK DIVISION)

WELL MET BY WITCHLIGHT 30p
Nina Beachcroft
0 426 10356 4 **A Target Adventure**
In which Sarah, Christopher and Lucy meet a strange little old woman called Mary, a 'white' witch who can tame animals, raise wind and water, change her shape and, yes—actually fly on a broomstick! Whether or not she can deal with the evil-eyed Mrs Bella Black, a very powerful 'black' witch who lives in the next village, is another matter which concerns the children very much as they are caught up into the middle of a terrifyingly dangerous battle fought out between the two witches on the supernatural plane.

THAT MAD, BAD BADGER 25p
Molly Burkett
0 426 10399 4
A blow-by-blow true account of life with 'Nikki' the badger, who delights in whipping laces out of the shoes of unsuspecting visitors to the Burkett household, stealing goodies from the 'fridge, and lying tummyside-up in a comfortable armchair for a quiet snooze. There have been other stories about badgers, but never one like this! *Illustrated.*

AWKWARD MAGIC 25p
Elisabeth Beresford
0 426 10153 7 **A Target Adventure**
Joe finds what he thinks is a dog being tormented by two boys in a Brighton basement area. No dog this, but a live Griffin, that fabulous beast of the Ancient World, whom Joe, and his young friend Grace, assist in searching for some lost treasure. . . . Magic and laughter make a happy mixture in this exciting book! *Illustrated.*

SEA-GREEN MAGIC 30p
Elisabeth Beresford
0 426 10479 x **A Target Adventure**
In which Johnny finds a funny, square-shaped bottle with a strange misty look about it whilst exploring sea-side rock pools. Imprisoned inside is an Arabian Djinn, or genie, who when released is destined to create some awkward problems for Johnny, Lorna and Alan. *Illustrated.*

HAUNTED HOUSES 30p

Bernhardt J. Hurwood

0 426 10559 1 **A Target Mystery**

Who was the ghost of Powis Castle? Why has he not been seen for 200 years? What was the cause of the fatal curse on Mouse Tower? And why does Anne Boleyn ride headless with a coach and four around the grounds of Blicking Hall? Here are 25 spine-chilling tales to spirit you away . . . into HAUNTED HOUSES! *Illustrated.*

FAMOUS HISTORICAL MYSTERIES 35p

Leonard Gribble

0 426 10428 5

Ten of the most famous and intriguing mysteries in international history, many of them still unsolved today. Try and discover the truth beneath the facts and fallacies which surround, among others: Anastasia, Princess of Russia; The Dreyfus Case; the disappearance of Amelia Earhart; the *Mary Celeste*, ghost-ship; and the secret identity of the Prisoner in the Iron Mask . . . *Illustrated.*

DOCTOR WHO AND THE ABOMINABLE SNOWMEN 30p

Terrance Dicks

0 426 10583 4

Why are the peaceful Yeti now spreading death and destruction? And what is the secret behind the glowing cave on the mountain? When DOCTOR WHO discovers that a long-dead friend is still alive, he *knows* why his visit to the lonely Himalayan monastery has led to a struggle to save the Earth! *Illustrated.*

DOCTOR WHO AND THE CYBERMEN 35p

Gerry Davis

0 426 10575 3

THE CYBERMEN have arrived. With metal limbs, they have the strength of ten men. They can live in the airless vacuum of space. They have no heart, no feelings, no emotions, and only one goal – power! In the year 2070, a small blue planet caught their attention. They would land, attack, ransack, destroy and finally abandon . . . Can DOCTOR WHO save the Earth and defeat an enemy whose threat is almost as great as that of the mighty Daleks? *Illustrated.*

SKIPPER—THE DOG FROM THE SEA 30p
Judith M. Berrisford
0 426 10487 0 **Target Animal Fiction**

A strange white Alsatian dog visits the Appleby seaside farmstead by moonlight. Whose dog is he? Will he make friends with the four Appleby children—Roddy, Jane, Kitty and Pete? What is the mystery behind him? The Appleby family have some exciting moments in this thrilling story before they find the answers to these questions. . . . *The first adventure in this famous series. Illustrated.*

SKIPPER TO THE RESCUE! 30p
Judith M. Berrisford
0 426 10495 1 **Target Animal Fiction**

Bad news! The Appleby farmstead is in danger of having to be sold off, so it's Skipper, Roddy, Jane, Kitty and Pete—to the rescue! Whilst the children are busy trying to raise money to help the farm out of its difficulties, Skipper does a little extra rescue work of his own and ends up winning the Blue Cross Medal! . . . *The second adventure in this famous series. Illustrated.*

AGATON SAX AND THE DIAMOND THIEVES 25p
Nils-Olof Franzen
0 426 10196 0 **Target Humour**

In which AGATON SAX, world famous newspaper-owner and amateur detective, pits his brilliant brain and iron nerve against the tough, unpleasant and horribly clever Octopus P. Scott in a bid to recover the priceless Koh-mih-Nor diamond . . . and Inspector Lispington of Scotland Yard gets a bucketful of cold porridge over his head! *Illustrated.*

AGATON SAX AND THE SCOTLAND YARD MYSTERY 25p
Nils-Olof Franzen
0 426 10209 6 **Target Humour**

In which AGATON SAX, Editor-in-Chief of the *Bykoping Post* and detective extraordinary, directs his amazing intelligence (and his editorial telescope) to the problem of who has stolen Scotland Yard's *Secret Code Register of Current Criminals* . . . the infamous crew of the bad ship *Esmeralda* lose their soup . . . and the mysterious 'Boss' gets a nasty shock to his system. *Illustrated.*

THE STORY OF THE LOCH NESS MONSTER 30p
Tim Dinsdale
0 426 10591 5 **A Target Mystery**
What mysterious entity lurks beneath the 1000 ft. deep, sinister-looking waters of Loch Ness in the Highlands of Scotland? Since the 1930s, men have sought the answer to this question. The author, a full-time, professional monster-hunter, tells you the history of the search for 'Nessie', and her cousin 'Morag', the monster of Loch Morar, and of the latest discoveries made with scientific equipment. *Fully illustrated with maps, photographs, and drawings.*

THE LONDON QUIZ BOOK 30p
R. W. Wilson
0 426 10436 6
Going on a day visit or holiday to London? Have fun by asking your friends, and yourself for that matter, questions about this most exciting of all the capital cities in the world! Questions on: Royal London; Government; Law and Order; museums; the Thames; zoos and parks; statues; famous buildings; ancient traditions and so forth . . . *Illustrated.*

THE GLORY HOUSE 25p
Charlotte Morrow
0 426 10225 8
Ever since Rose first discovered the remote, long-deserted house on the gorse-covered heathland above her home, she has gained strange comfort from the dreams she weaves around it . . . until, that is, she encounters the occupants of Mill Cottage and with them a threat to her world of make-believe. *Illustrated.*

STONE OF TERROR 30p
Margaret Greaves
0 426 10305 x
A tale of young love and witchcraft for older readers in which Philip Hoskyn befriends young Marie Perchon, niece of Annette Perchon—outcast, witch and priestess of the terrifying *Grandmother Stone*. Can Marie and Philip survive its malevolent influence?

If you enjoyed this book and would like to have information sent you about other TARGET titles, write to the address below.

You will also receive:

A FREE TARGET BADGE!

Based on the TARGET BOOKS symbol—see front cover of this book—this attractive three-colour badge, pinned to your blazer-lapel, or jumper, will excite the interest and comment of all your friends!

and you will be further entitled to:

FREE ENTRY INTO THE TARGET DRAW!

All you have to do is cut off the coupon beneath, write on it your name and address *in block capitals*, and pin it to your letter. You will be advised of your lucky draw number. Twice a year, in June and December, numbers will be drawn 'from the hat' and the winner will receive a complete year's set of TARGET books.

Write to: TARGET BOOKS,
Universal-Tandem Publishing Co.,
14 Gloucester Road,
London SW7 4RD

——————— cut here ———————

Full name..

Address...

....

...............................County...

Age...............................